GENERATIVITY

Andrew Lynn has a Ph.D. in Renaissance literature from Cambridge University. He now works to help resolve international and cross-border disputes.

www.andrewlynn.com

GENERATIVITY

THE ART AND SCIENCE OF EXCEPTIONAL ACHIEVEMENT

ANDREW LYNN

HOWGILL
HOUSE

Howgill House Books

www.howgillhousebooks.com

Copyright © Andrew Lynn 2017

ISBN 978-1-912360-01-7

CONTENTS

INTRODUCTION

THE PROPOSITION

This is a radical book.

It's radical in two ways. In the first place, it's radical in the commonplace, everyday meaning of the term. It's radical in the sense that what is contained within is unabashedly disrespectful of the conventional way in which we approach knowledge in this fragmented, technocratic, and hyper-specialized age.

It's also radical in another sense – the word *radical* coming from the Latin *radix* (meaning 'root' or 'going to the origin'). It's radical not only in that the ideas advanced find their origin in the wisdom of many generations and civilizations, but also in that its core proposition is one that would have been generally approved in virtually every human era other than our own.

The proposition is a bare one – that the great work is not the work of changing the world but of changing oneself.

This naked proposition is found in ancient Rome in the words of Marcus Aurelius: 'The universe is change; our life is what our thoughts make it.' It is found in the words of the Gnostic Christ: 'For whoever does not know self, does not know anything, but whoever knows self, already has acquired knowledge about the depth of the universe.' It is found in the ancient philosophy of the Far East: 'Mastering others is strength; mastering yourself is true power.' It is found in thirteenth-century Persia in the Sufi poet Rumi: 'Why should I seek? I am the same as he. His essence speaks through me. I have been looking for myself!' It is found in India in the independence period in the words of Gandhi: 'If we could change ourselves, the tendencies in the world would also change.' And it is found in a sentiment attributed to the great humanitarian Mother Theresa: 'If everyone only cleaned their own doorstep, the whole world would be clean.'

When I started my enquiries, I hadn't been of this view. Like many young researchers of my generation, my education had taken place in the shadow of post-1960s educational reform and social change. What this meant was that well before the point of my entering university, the dominant perspective upon the study of the humanities had been materialism or one of its many subvariants. It seemed that wherever I looked, 'great men' were under attack: in history, Thomas Carlyle's view that 'the history of the world is but the biography of great men' received at best short shrift and at worst vitriolic abuse; in philosophy, philosopher kings were giving way to the history of ideas; and, less flatteringly still, 'dead white men', as they called them, had become the *bêtes noires* of my own first discipline (literature). Social structures and ideology replaced living human beings. Undergraduate work consisted far more of Karl Marx than it did *Bhagavad Gita*.

At Cambridge my research focused on greatness in literature: why, for instance, is Shakespeare considered to be a truly great, 'universal' writer, whereas his rivals fall by the wayside? In line with some of the presuppositions I had absorbed from my undergraduate days, I looked to the surrounding context and the context of readers and audiences for an explanation: was there something in their social, political, or economic structure that had made Shakespeare's work more compelling than that of his contemporaries? For three years I rummaged through the manuscripts and early printed books of the seventeenth century, looking for evidence as to the effect of England's bloody civil wars, regicide, restoration, and Glorious Revolution. There was no better place to do this: Cambridge, then as now, has some of the world's best minds at work on similar projects, in an environment that is beyond enchanting.

I now think this approach was wrong. There probably are modest 'socio-economic' aspects in the development and assessment of great individuals. But 'greatness' by definition has a quality that is rare if not unique – a quality that cannot be merely the product of the age. Either we get rid of the concept of greatness altogether, then, or we start looking for its personal, individual components. Of no less importance was the realization – which had come to me more strongly on leaving academia for the law – that we are at our best when we call upon our own resources as individuals, rather than always looking to society for answers.

When my work began, I started out looking at the nature of exceptional creativity. As I dug deeper, that extended into all areas of human activity. What is truly of interest, I concluded, is the fortuitous coming together of multiple factors that constitutes the common wellspring of human productivity. This I call 'generativity', and it has been the task of this book to explore it.

I believe this needs to be done *holistically*. But how? Well, sometimes great people are kind enough to tell us how they did it: they leave autobiographies, or interviews, or other records. Here, you will find me raiding biographies of Pablo Picasso and Muhammad Ali, for example, as well as interviews with free soloist John Bachar and diary extracts from Van Gogh. Sometimes we have research – psychological, sociological, biological, and historical. So here you'll also find me delving into a good number of research findings on the 'new' unconscious, selective perception, scientific lineage, cognitive complexity, expertise, life span, and cumulative advantage, among others. Last but far from least, sometimes we have insight from traditional wisdom and classic literature. And here, you will find me drawing upon a diverse range of sources from scholars and philosophers to poets and artists and the tellers of folktales.

In addition to being done holistically, I also believe this needs to be done *selectively*. We live in an era of information overload. We are not starved of information, but gorged with it. The role of the writer, the scholar, and the public intellectual has changed; it is no longer primarily to transmit knowledge, but to organize it. The French mathematician and philosopher Blaise Pascal said in one of his *Lettres Provinciales*: 'I have made this longer than usual because I have not had time to make it shorter.' It has taken a lot of time to get the book you hold in your hands as short as it is now.

Chapter One deals with what I call 'inner state'. The ancient Zoroastrians, I suggest, had it right: we are best served by starting from the 'inside out' – going from good thoughts to good words to good deeds – rather than the other way around. We will find here that experts have a cognitive advantage over non-experts and quite literally *see* their respective fields differently – and with more precision – than the rest of us. We will explore Muhammad Ali's great surprise triumph over George Foreman in Zaire in 1974 and what it tells us about the power of strong internal sense of reality (or 'frame'). We will then go on to consider what Dostoevsky's *The Idiot* has to say about the relative merits of imagination and intention. Truly generative people, we will discover, have found ways of interpreting and manifesting their own reality in ways that are most productive to them.

In Chapter Two, our attention shifts to a neglected aspect of human activity – the regulation of energy. In the words of the great revolutionary poet and artist William Blake, 'energy is eternal delight'. There are at least two reasons to think Blake may have been on to something. The first is that we know creativity has Darwinian aspects: it happens through a trial-and-error process that rewards boldness and lack of initial inhibition. And the second is a result of the inner resource we draw upon when exercising willpower or making choices. Self-control, we find out, has its costs: it's a limited resource that needs to be conserved. Highly generative people know how to do that.

Chapter Three is all about the effect of other people. It explains why husbands and wives come to look like each other and why you're more likely to be overweight if you have overweight friends. More importantly, it reveals how scientific and artistic generativity is determined by mentors and patrons as well as influential predecessors several generations back in time. There could have been no Goya without Velázquez and Rembrandt, I suggest in this chapter, and Wordsworth wouldn't have been Wordsworth had he not been inspired by John Milton from almost two centuries before.

In Chapter Four, it is not the resting state but the engaged state that we consider. Our focus here is on the 'now'. We see that artists, climbers, and mystics (among others) share a common absorption in the immediate performance of what they are doing. This is a state that has been identified in religious texts already thousands of years old and restated more recently in the terms of modern science.

Chapter Five concerns the intellect. In this chapter we see how eminence has historically been related to advocating minority viewpoints: great men and women have tended to be unrepresentative of the spirit of their age, inconsistent, and reactionary. We also see how successful political leaders show high levels of 'cognitive complexity' – they are able to see the merits of multiple points of view at the same time. And we agree with Søren Kierkegaard that the secret is all about cultivating a habit of seeing things with fresh, unsullied eyes.

In Chapter Six, we discover how to become an expert. We look at how much time it takes and the life span curves that tell us at what point we're likely to do out greatest work. Here we probe right into the nature of expertise by looking at chess masters to identify the 'cognitive advantage' experts have over the rest of us. We close by considering the achingly beautiful *Sorrow* and *The Roots* of Van Gogh – in the light of what he has told us in his diaries about the circumstances of their creation – to identify what is necessary to take the step from 'mere' expertise to undisputed genius.

We end in Chapter Seven on the topic of 'serendipity', asking why some people, seemingly as a result of chance or arbitrary good fortune, do so much better than others. We find an answer in the operation of cumulative advantage, a process by which small advantages snowball into great differences in outcome. We see – by reference to the performance of American schoolchildren and by reference to the success story of the Jewish people – how this deep principle underpins the lives of individuals and peoples alike.

Writing on this topic was always bound to be a humbling experience. While we can increasingly trace many of the causes and conditions of personal achievement, its very deepest roots remain shrouded in mystery. That is as it should be. Part of the beauty of a Mozart concerto or a Michelangelo painting is in the miracle of it all. Attempting to explain them as we would explain the workings of a combustion engine or a clockwork doll would only cause some of that magic to be lost.

If what you want is a mechanical 'how to' guide, then, please put this book down now – you will only be disappointed. If, on the other hand, what you are seeking is an open-minded and curious exploration of the many hidden wellsprings of human generativity – then read on.

This book may just be for you.

INNER STATE

THE SECRET GOSPELS

In Zoroastrianism, the old Persian religion predating Islam, there is a saying: *humata, hukhta, hvarshta* – 'good thoughts, good words, good deeds'. What on the surface seems like a simple statement of basic morality actually carries with it a profound message. *Humata* is defined as the primeval creative thought of Ahura Mazda, the supreme creator god. *Hukhta* stands for holy words of prayer that contribute to the ongoing creation of the world. *Hvarshta* are the acts that move us forward to our life's purpose.[1] The gist is clear. Thoughts and words, as much as actions, are creative: they set in motion chains of cause and effect the outcome of which can be far-reaching. 'Watch your thoughts, for they become words,' goes the modern equivalent. 'Watch your words, for they become actions. Watch your actions, for they become habits. Watch your habits, for they become your character. And watch your character, for it becomes your destiny. What we think, we become.'

The Zoroastrian saying highlights a principle that has long been at the heart of several of the great spiritual traditions of mankind – although it is admittedly more commonly encountered in neglected, heretical, or esoteric circles than in the religious mainstream.

It can be found in the secret gospels of gnostic Christianity, for example, the most significant of which were unearthed by accident in 1945 where they had been buried near the city of Nag Hammadi on the west banks of the Nile. Gnostic Christianity postulated not one but two gods: the good, true God far above and a lower, evil deity and maker of this world, identified as the God of the Old Testament. Gnosticism stressed direct inner experience of the divine light within, which was to be freed from its enslavement in the material world. In the *Gospel According to Thomas*, which had been found at Nag Hammadi, the Gnostic Christ expressed the core of his philosophy this way: 'If you bring forth what is within you, what you bring forth will save you. If you do not bring forth what is within you, what you do not bring forth will destroy you.'[2]

Sufism – the inner mystical tradition of Islam – expresses a similar vision. For the Sufis, mankind is engaged in a struggle with the lower dimension of his existence – the animal energies called *nafs*. As described by the great Sufi poet Rumi, the *nafs* are like a dog in a doorway who not only attacks visitors coming in but also prevents the owner moving freely too. Fighting this inner battle is what Rumi elsewhere has called the 'lesser jihad'. To do that effectively means controlling thoughts, moods, reading, conversation, and whole intake of mental 'food'. Whatever we keep hidden in our hearts God manifests in us outwardly. 'Whenever you entrust your heart to a thought,' wrote Rumi in the *Masnavi*, 'something will be taken from you inwardly.'[3]

The principle is even reiterated in certain of the remote schools of Tibetan Buddhism – for example, in the Madhyamika ('Middle Way') school founded by Nagarjuna based upon sutras said to have been the words of the Buddha lost to mankind for many centuries. According to the Madhyamika, the very base of human experience is nothing more than the fugitive contact by our senses with one stimulus or another. There are, accordingly, two worlds: the world of pure contact not coloured by the screen of memories, and the world created by mental formations known as *samskaras*. The second of these is the world that we live in. 'It is thus that a kind of illusory reality is given to the world which we build up in holding it to be exterior to ourselves, whereas it emanates from us and dwells in us in dependence on the illusion of which we are the victims.'[4]

The message of this chapter draws upon these realizations but extends them in a new direction. We

11

will find that people of unusually high levels of generativity work, like our good Zoroastrians, from the inside out. They are able to comprehend that the world is part perceived and part created. As the part that does the creating is under their own control, they then regulate their underlying state. The very best of them at the highest level become meaning-makers, transforming the way that they understand the world so as to thrive when times are good and survive when they are not.

THE COGNITIVE ADVANTAGE OF EXPERTS

Exceptional people focus, whether knowingly or unknowingly, on aspects of their reality that help them and interpret that reality in ways that are productive. The phenomenon can be seen broadly, but there's nowhere where it has been demonstrated more definitely than in sports. This isn't just a matter of positive thinking. It's a matter of literally perceiving reality differently – in a way that is fresh and beneficial. The shift in perception that occurs at elite levels in sports can be readily illustrated by recent work on what makes a top performer in cricket.

At its highest levels, cricket is a ferociously demanding game. At international levels the ball can be bowled at speeds of up to 160 km/hour – that's almost 45 metres per second. What that means is that the ball can travel the distance between bowler and batsman in less than 500 ms. To put that in perspective, the sum total of the reaction time of the batsman (perhaps 200 ms) and the movement time of legs and bat (perhaps 700 ms) is approximately 900 ms.[5]

And it's not just about the speed. Professional bowlers have an arsenal of balls they can throw at you. The ball can be made to deviate in the air as it approaches (outswinger/inswinger) or after it bounces (leg-spinner/wrong-un). Balls can be thrown full length (so that they bounce close to the batsman) or short (so that they bounce closer to the bowler). Whatever the ball, the batsman has to be there for it: positional errors have to be kept beneath 5 cm and timing errors beneath a miniscule 2 to 3 ms for successful bat-ball contact.

None of that, though, should distract from the central problem: it takes 900 ms to respond to an event that occurs in the space of a mere 500 ms. You don't need to be a mathematician to see that – at some level – the best professional batsmen have mastered the art of the impossible.

How, then, do world-class batsmen do it? If it is impossible to rely on reaction time alone, then what gives them their edge?

A team of Australian scholars led by Sean Müller went about exploring this. They filmed the actions of two bowlers (one a medium-pace swing bowler and the second a leg-spin bowler) as they bowled a series of different deliveries. The bowlers were instructed to deliver three sets of different ball types: an outswinger, inswinger, and short ball for the swing bowler; and a leg-spinner, 'wrong-un', and short ball for the spin bowler. The video clips of these images were digitally edited to create a total of ninety-six 'trials' (forty-eight trials for each bowler).

The participants in the experiment came from three groups of varying levels of expertise. One group was composed of 'highly skilled' players: these were recruited from the cricket squads of the Australian Test, Queensland Bulls First Class, Queensland Academy of Sport, and Australian Institute of Sport. The second group was composed of 'intermediate players' recruited from the Queensland Cricket Association third grade competition. University students made up the final group of 'low skilled' players.

Players from each of the three groups were shown the clips (projected at a size of 1.78 × 1.38 m) and asked to predict both ball type and ball length. There was, however, one additional difficulty. The images were hidden (or 'occluded') at certain moments in the delivery and the participants would be required to make their prediction on the basis of information available to them up to that point. Sometimes they would be shown the whole delivery and make their predictions on that basis. In other trials the image would be occluded at ball release, at first-foot impact (FFI), and even as early in delivery as back-foot impact (BFI).

The results? Starting with the swing bowler trials, a curious pattern began to emerge. Players of all ability levels displayed a respectable ability to predict the type and length of ball when they were able to see the full video clip from run-up to release and beyond. Where the highly skilled batsmen have a unique advantage, however, is that they were able to predict the type of ball that would be coming their way even when ball flight information was occluded. The expert batsmen showed an even more pronounced ability to predict the type of ball well before it had been released (i.e., somewhere between BFI and FFI).

What that means is that somewhere between

and

and at the very least between this

and this

the expert batsman has been able to extract and act upon some reasonably accurate information that the others were not able to capitalize upon. Simply put, great batsmen are able to anticipate the type and trajectory of the ball well before it has even left the bowler's hand.

Müller and his colleagues then took the experiment a bit further to establish what precisely it was that the world-class batsmen were seeing that the rest of us – you, me, the university students, and even intermediate players – seem to be missing. It's this:

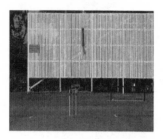

The bowler's head, torso, legs, and non-bowling arm and hand have been occluded. All that is left of the bowler is his bowling arm and hand in the pre-release stage. Guess what? If an expert batsman sees only this, he can still predict at accuracy levels significantly greater than chance what kind of ball will be coming his way.[6]

———

The idea that exceptional people perceive an alternative heightened 'reality' conflicts, of course, with the commonsense belief that the objective world 'just is'. Samuel Johnson once famously attempted to refute the idealistic philosophy of Bishop Berkeley in the simplest way possible – by kicking against a large stone with such force that his foot rebounded from it. It's no surprise that scientists have for a long time been broadly of Johnson's camp. Sensory stimulation, it was thought, triggered neurological events that in turn gave rise to perception. The act of perception itself was considered to be essentially passive.

There has, however, been a problem with this model. If it were indeed the case that perception is passive, people wearing light-reversing goggles would experience an inversed perceptual image of the world. But that isn't what happens. In fact, people who wear the goggles for some time and intentionally interact with the world come to perceive a normal image of it. Even at this most basic level of raw perception, then, the mind is busy rearranging the information transmitted by the senses.

In the same way that active perception can 'fill in' and make up for objective perceptual deficiencies, so inactive perception can erase or distort aspects of the environment that are objectively present. We suffer from change blindness: experiments have shown that people don't notice when looking at a picture that the men in that picture have had their hats exchanged – an effect that occurred for fully 100 percent of observers – and we don't notice when one individual is replaced by another wearing different clothes. We also suffer from inattentional blindness: while watching a group of people passing a ball to each other, observers have failed to notice a person dressed as a black gorilla walking straight through the group. And it goes further. Our subjective conditions don't just blind us to aspects of reality, they also contaminate the world as we experience it. Those who fear heights perceive ledges as higher than those with less fear. Hills appear steeper for tired, elderly, unfit, and unhealthy people, as well as for those bearing heavy loads.[7]

The world presented to us by our perceptions does not, in fact, need to be anything like reality. Darwinists may say that perceptions accurately reflect reality and that there is a good reason for this. 'Obviously we must be latching onto reality in some way because otherwise we would have been wiped out a long time ago,' runs this line of thinking. 'If I think I'm seeing a palm tree but it's really a tiger, I'm in trouble.' Evolutionary fitness, though, doesn't require that we know the world accurately; it merely requires that the way we perceive the world contributes to survival and reproduction. David Hoffman of the University of California, Irvine, compares this to use of icons on a computer: it doesn't matter that an icon doesn't look anything like the innards of the computer where the corresponding file is stored; all that matters is that the icon functions as a useful guide. Evolution 'has shaped us with perceptions that allow us to survive,' says Hoffman.

'But part of that involves hiding from us the stuff we don't need to know. And that's pretty much all of reality, whatever reality might be. If you had to spend all that time figuring it out,' he adds, 'the tiger would eat you.'[8]

The German-Swiss writer Herman Hesse spoke of this power of the mind in one of his most enigmatic works, *Demian* (1919), by reference to the unusual lovemaking abilities of the night-moth. There is a species of night-moth, says Hesse, in which the females are much less common than the males. If you take a female night-moth of this species, the male moths sense her as the only female in the region and will visit from hours away – even at a distance of several miles. 'Nature abounds with such inexplicable things,' he concludes. 'But my argument is: if the female moths were as abundant as the males, the latter would not have such a highly developed sense of smell. They've acquired it only because they had to train themselves to have it.' The male night-moths need to obtain a certain outcome; they therefore need to have the means to achieve the outcome; nature then rises to the task and provides it for them. The need brings outs the potentiality. Hesse draws the inevitable parallel: 'If a person were to concentrate all his will power on a certain end, then he would achieve it.'

———

Expert athletes in fast ball sports are somewhat like Hesse's night-moths. They don't necessarily have a physical advantage over the rest of us; research has shown that top athletes do not, in fact, possess faster reaction times than members of the general population. What they have is a *cognitive advantage*. They are able to use body cues (rather than just ball trajectory) to predict the nature of the shots they will face and to take appropriate action on that basis. Expert athletes make more effective use of information from the visual field than do relative novices.[9]

FRAME

The research shows that perception changes – it heightens and becomes more precisely attuned to important features – as expertise grows. Where it is silent is on whether we can take deliberate steps to adjust the way we perceive the field of our activities – and if so, how? For that, we can examine what some of the really great athletes themselves have said and done.

Not many sporting events compare with the 1974 fight between Muhammad Ali and George Foreman in Kinshasa. The fight, which would come to be known as the 'Rumble in the Jungle', was considered to be a historic event and has been called 'arguably the greatest sporting event of the twentieth century'.[10] It was not, however, a fight that Ali was tipped to win. Foreman was younger, looked fitter, and was indisputably stronger. He had won all of his forty previous fights, thirty-seven of them by knockout. If Foreman was on the way up, it looked like Ali was on the way down. After three-and-one-half years' suspension for refusal to comply with the draft, he had failed so far to recover the title that had been stripped from him.

From the outset, though, it becomes clear that this is no ordinary fight. The bell rings and Ali charges forward to meet a slower moving but equally resolute Foreman. Foreman presses Ali back. After circling and feinting, Ali fires out a light left jab, then a hard right into the centre of Foreman's forehead. It connects. Ali dances around Foreman. Around fifteen seconds later Ali strikes home again – with another right. The pattern is set; Ali has been hitting with right-hand leads. This is the most dangerous and difficult punch – a result of the fact that the right hand has a lot farther to travel, exposing the fighter to counterattacks from the left. 'Champions do not hit other champions with right-hand leads.'[11]

Foreman recovers his composure in the ensuing rounds imposing upon Ali with his sheer physical strength. Then – in round 7 with Ali up against the ropes and taking a pounding from Foreman – something totally unexpected happens: Ali starts talking to his opponent. He would later recall the episode like this:

> I said, "Okay sucker, I'm backing up against the ropes, and I want you to take your best shots." And I just stood there. "Come on, show me something. Show me something, kid. You're not doing nothing. You're just a girl, look at you. You ain't got nothing. Come on sucker, show me something. Show me something, sucker."

What happens next is there for all to see in video recordings of the fight. Foreman keeps coming with punches: a right uppercut to the body, cross, jab and cross, and several body hooks – all with Ali simply taking the blows. 'He was so tired,' remembers Ali in an interview he gave later, 'he was just falling on the ropes. I said, "Man, this is the *wrong* place to get tired."' Foreman recalls the fight in similar terms: 'All he would say is: "Is that all you got, George?" And that,' says Foreman, 'was about all I had.'

This interchange would be the turning point of

the fight. The instant Ali got off the ropes he threw a lightning fast and devastating combination of blows, knocking Foreman to the ground and out for the count. The episode was totally unexpected and would change Foreman's world forever. Ali had in effect overpowered his opponent not only with his physical force, but also with the force of his own reality. 'I went out to beat and destroy a boxer,' reflected Foreman later. 'Little did I know I would be facing something greater than a boxer.'

The firmness of mind Ali showed at the critical moment can be called 'frame'. Frames, according to cognitive scientists, are mental structures that shape the way we see the world – our goals, actions, values, and sense of reality.[12] Frames were originally studied from a linguistic standpoint, and most framing theory has been directed at creating persuasive communications. This is because every word evokes a frame, and so the use of words to evoke preferred frames has been a centre of attention for linguists and communications experts. 'Frame' singular, however, refers to a much broader and deeper concept: the coherence of a person's subjective reality. A strong or robust frame is one that retains coherence in the face of external shocks, whether from circumstances or people.

———

Can we reconstruct how Ali may have cultivated his impregnable 'frame' in the fight against Foreman in Zaire? One September afternoon seven weeks before the fight in Kinshasa, the American writer Norman Mailer had taken a trip to Ali's training camp at Deer Lake, Pennsylvania. Deer Lake is famous both for its replicas of slave cabins high on the hill as well as boulders on the entrance road painted with the names of Ali's opponents. The mood had been gloomy as Ali prepared to face the man widely perceived to be his greatest challenge yet. Just a few months earlier, Foreman had destroyed Ken Norton in a fight in Caracas, knocking him down for the second time in only the second round and landing no fewer than five blows as he fell – 'as quick in the instant as a lion slashing its prey', as Mailer put it.

In spite of this, Ali cultivated an unshakeable self-confidence. Every day he would subject his interviewers to the same speeches, the same poems, and the same mock punches flashed two inches short of their face. 'One whole horrendous nightmare – Foreman's extermination of Norton – was being converted, reporter by reporter, poem by poem, same analysis after same analysis – "He's got a hard-push punch but he can't *hit*" – into the reinstallation of Ali's ego.' A great fighter will not live with anxiety like other men, thought Mailer; to think of how much he can be hurt by another fighter would make him not more creative but less. Buried anxiety, Mailer suggested, was transmuted to ego. 'What a wall of ego Ali's will had erected over the years.'[13]

———

A further clue comes from what happened shortly before that fight. Before travelling to the stadium, Ali had asked to speak on the phone to the legendary boxing trainer Cus D'Amato. D'Amato had been Ali's boxing mentor, and in this moment he focussed on the psychological aspect of the fight. Ali was to throw his first punch 'with bad intentions', instructed D'Amato. 'Fear is like fire,' added D'Amato, 'it can burn your house down or it can cook your food.'[14]

We don't know, beyond this, exactly how D'Amato might have helped to strengthen Ali's frame prior to the Foreman fight. We do know, however, how D'Amato worked with the boxer widely considered to be second only to Ali in the history of boxing – Mike Tyson. What Tyson tells us about D'Amato's approach is unusually revealing as to how champions are made.

At the beginning, D'Amato didn't even let Tyson box. Instead, after a workout, he would sit down with Tyson and they would talk. 'He'd talk about my feelings and emotions and about the psychology of boxing. He wanted to reach me at the root,' recalled Tyson afterwards. 'We talked a lot about the spiritual aspects of the game.' 'If you don't have the spiritual warrior in you,' D'Amato told his young protégé, 'you'll never be a fighter. I don't care how big and strong you are.'

The approach taken shows us how a resilient 'frame' can be built up.

First, the starting point was to be the mind. The mind, for D'Amato, was nothing less than a battleground. 'Your mind is not your friend, Mike. I hope you know that. You have to fight with your mind, control it, put it in its place. You have to control your emotions. Fatigue in the ring is 90 percent psychological. It's just the excuse of a man who wants to quit.' Sometimes D'Amato would say to Tyson, 'You allow your mind to get the better of you' – unlike the greatest fighters who 'could fight the best fight of their life even if someone had just kidnapped their child or killed their mother.' D'Amato 'thought that punching hard had nothing to do with anything physical, it was all emotional. Controlled emotion.'

Second, D'Amato set out to release some of Tyson's limiting beliefs: 'My job is to peel off layers and layers of damages that are inhibiting your true ability to grow and fulfill your potential.' It's clear enough that the 'peeling off' was actually a breaking down of inner limitations. 'No one ever made me more conscious of being a black man,' said Tyson. At the same time, D'Amato would remind Tyson that

27

nothing could stop him but himself: 'You're so superior to those people. They can never do what you are capable of doing. You got it in you.' D'Amato was dredging up and disposing of Tyson's mental effluvia and inner resistance. 'You could conquer any world. Don't use the word "can't." You can't say "can't."'

Third, D'Amato went about remodelling the inner man. The method adopted for Tyson was inspired by the work of an early twentieth-century French pharmacist and psychologist by the name of Emile Coué. Coué had developed a method of self-suggestion based upon the idea that the unconscious presides over all our actions, and that we reach the unconscious and direct its purposes by active imagination and autosuggestion. Autosuggestion is not a choice, thought Coué; it happens anyway as a result of the way our minds work. The choice is as to *what kind* of autosuggestions we want floating around in our heads.

D'Amato had a copy of Coué's work and had managed – using its methods – to reverse the effects of a cataract on his eyesight. He was determined to apply this method to Tyson. The classic Coué affirmation is to say, 'Every day in every way, getting better and better'. D'Amato had Tyson modify this. 'So he had me saying, "The best fighter in the world. Nobody can beat me" over and over again all day. I loved doing that, I loved hearing myself talking about myself.' But none of this came automatically; it came, recalls

Tyson, from repeatedly going over the visualization in your mind.[15]

To reinforce this, there was deliberate modeling on eminent predecessors. The list is extensive. Tyson chatted with Muhammad Ali in October 1980, after prompting from D'Amato. His favourite boxer, however, was Roberto Duran ('I was short and ugly and I had a speech impediment ... *Man this guy is me*, I thought. He was not ashamed of being who he was.') Tyson also fell in love with Jack Johnson ('I loved his arrogance'). After moving in with D'Amato, he spent time reading the boxing encyclopedia and watching old fight films for up to ten hours a day.

It was all about entering into the world of the great fighters, mentally becoming them in order to lay the foundation for his own victories. Tyson is explicit about this in his memoirs: 'I was serious about my history because I learned so much from the old fighters. What did I have to do to be like this guy? Cus would tell me how vicious and mean they were outside the ring but when they're in it, they're relaxed and calm. . . . I would watch the fights on TV and I'd see the boxers punching with grimaces on their faces and their ripped bodies, and I wanted that to be my face and my body.'[16]

This is an approach that pre-empts much of the

recent research on the relationship between mental state and performance.

It's now well known, for instance, that we can be 'primed' through exposure to certain words or images to respond in predictable ways – without even necessarily knowing about it. Expose people to a set of key words designed to bring about a high-performance goal (e.g., win, compete, succeed, strive, attain, achieve, and master) on a word-search puzzle, for example, and they will respond by better solving the puzzle. Participants in these studies are, however, not only *not* aware of the impact of the priming, but they are also not aware that there had been any priming going on at all. Most 'appeared perplexed' by the suggestion that the priming may have influenced their behaviour.[17]

It's also known that certain mental images can also improve outcomes. People who have been asked merely to imagine a typical professor for five minutes (listing such things as behaviour, lifestyle, and appearance) have tended to perform better at general knowledge questions than people who have been asked to imagine a typical secretary. This doesn't require anything as fanciful as actually making someone instantaneously more intelligent. It could instead be that people allocate their effort differently, perhaps by concentrating harder. It could also be that people are induced to use smarter and more varied problem-solving strategies. Or it could even be that people have an altered 'feeling for knowing' and so may use their knowledge differently (e.g., more confidently).[18]

Finally, we are in the process of finding out more about the significance of self-stereotyping. At one time it had been assumed that self-stereotypes were detrimental. Recent research suggests that this isn't necessarily the case, especially because most of us have multiple identities and in any one situation at least one of those identities may facilitate performance. So, for example, when female Asian American undergraduates had their *female* identity activated, they tended to underperform a mathematics test relative to a control group, but when they had their *Asian* identity made salient, they tended to outperform the group.[19]

Finding – or cultivating – the right identity is not only a matter of personal pride and wellbeing. It is also one of the keys to peak performance.

ANTI-FRAME

The concept of 'frame' can be used to describe the coherence of a person's subjective reality, especially when under threat and especially when such coherence is productive. One's 'frame' can be stronger or weaker according to the strength or weakness of the coherency. There is, however, a particular type of *in*coherency that has been observed by nineteenth-century commentators and reiterated in recent research. For convenience let's call this 'anti-frame'. What we mean by this can be best illustrated by a scene from Dostoevsky's *The Idiot*.[20]

An evening gathering has been arranged at a villa owned by the Yepanchins, minor figures in Russian high society. They invite to the party individuals whom they take to be the *crème-de-la-crème* of the national elite. There is Princess Belokonskaya, the central figure in this refined and elaborate world. There is an influential army general with a German name; he has attained one of the highest positions of the land and the wealth that goes with it, despite having no great achievements to his name (although once in five years he would offer a dictum 'remarkable for its profundity'.) There is a middle-aged nobleman of rank and high birth – a great talker with a reputation as a malcontent and the habits of an English gentleman. There is Prince N, a wealthy and splendid-looking nobleman and also a seducer and conqueror of female hearts across Europe. And there is a smattering of middling people like the Yepanchins themselves, looking to establish their place in this exclusive little world.

It's all been perfectly arranged. But there's a problem.

The problem comes in the form of one Prince

Myshkin. Myshkin is an idealistic young nobleman who has inherited a fortune – but he's also an idiot. Afflicted by illness, he has spent his formative years in Swiss clinic away from the temptations of society; he is a naïf who has never had to make compromises. He's what the Russians call a *yurodivy*, or a 'holy fool', a man whose simplicity proclaims his closeness to God. His idiocy is not a lack of intelligence or knowledge. On the contrary, he's remarkably eloquent and well informed. His idiocy is that he *tries too hard*.

Myshkin's fiancée, Aglaya, has tried to warn him. She has been worried about him making a fool of himself (and her) at the gathering. For some reason her fears begin to centre on a particular Chinese vase that has been placed in the Yepanchins' drawing room. It's a valuable item and a present – and she knows that if it were damaged there would be severe consequences. She warns Myshkin about it in no uncertain terms; he vows to sit absolutely as far away from it as possible. *The vase must not be damaged*, he tells himself. But he's afraid. Now that the vase has been mentioned, it's in his head and he has a sense of foreboding that he will do something to bring it tottering to the ground.

The gathering starts well. Myshkin is on his best behaviour: he's been warned, remember – and he has sat himself just as far away from the site of danger as he can get. The guests start mingling, however, and Myshkin is drawn into the conversation.

Inadvertently, he moves his seat nearer to the huge and beautiful Chinese vase. It's standing on a plinth more or less at a level with his elbow and, by now, just behind.

Conversation flows and the gathering comes alive. Myshkin's getting carried away with it all. He rises from his seat. He waves his arm carelessly. He moves his shoulder – and...

The vase totters and falls. The little German sitting there leaps away from its path and it smashes onto the floor. Then: a crash, shouting, precious shards on the floor, and astonishment from all around. Time stops for Myshkin. He stands there like a man apart – like a man watching from a distance an event that has no connection with himself. He sees the commotion and the fragments being cleared away and hears the sound of rapid conversation. The one thing he set out to avoid is the one thing that has happened. He has broken the vase.

———

What Dostoevsky is showing is something profound: that what is *attended* (the possible falling of the vase) trumps what is *intended* (doing whatever necessary to prevent it). What Myshkin fell afoul of at the dinner party was, in fact, a tendency of the human mind to bring into being precisely the opposite of what was intended by inadvertently fixating on it. There's a name for this: *ironic process*.

There's a classic and easily demonstrable example of an ironic process. It's disarmingly simple. All you need to do is this: try not to think of a white bear.

You will probably have found that task a little harder than you might initially have thought. If so, you wouldn't be alone. In tests where participants were asked to do precisely the same thing over a five-minute period, the average reporting of 'white bear thoughts' was 6.15. That means that they thought of a white bear more than once every minute. Compare that with the number of times you think of a white bear in your day-to-day life and you see the point. It would be very unusual for a typical individual (working outside a zoo) to think of a bear one time in a month. Thinking of a white bear one time a week would be exceptional. But one time *every minute?*

———

In fact, similar ironic effects have been found across a whole range of mental activities: concentration (subjects asked to remember cities on a map remembering the cities they had *not* been asked to focus attention upon), mood control (subjects asked to try *not* to feel unhappy feeling unhappier), intentional relaxation (subjects instructed to relax ending up with reduced relaxation levels), sleep (subjects told to try to sleep taking twice as long to fall asleep as those with no instructions), belief and disbelief (subjects believing marketing messages when instructed to disbelieve and *vice versa*), pain control (subjects experiencing greater pain perception when they tried to suppress pain than when they tried to distract themselves), and self-presentation (liars found to be less successful when strongly motivated to lie).[21]

Nothing here contradicts the main proposition of this chapter – that inner state determines experience of reality. Bur this inner state is not reducible to the limited and arid act of merely intending an outcome. It comprehends the whole imaginative inner world. In the words of Coué, 'When the imagination and willpower are in conflict, are antagonistic, it is always the imagination which wins'.[22]

THE DROWNED AND THE SAVED

When Primo Levi, survivor of the concentration camps, reflected upon his experience, he concluded that all men had fallen ultimately into one of two camps: the drowned and the saved.[23]

Levi had not been untroubled by the question of

what was to be gained by looking back upon the horrors and brutalities of that experience. But he acknowledged that there was, all the same, something very important to be learned from the camps. 'Thousands of individuals,' he wrote, 'differing in age, condition, origin, language, culture and customs, are enclosed within barbed wire: there they live a regular, controlled life which is identical for all and inadequate to all needs, and which is more rigorous than any experimenter could have set up to establish what is essential and what adventitious to the conduct of the human animal in the struggle for life.' The concentration camp had inadvertently become, he suggests, a 'gigantic biological and social experiment'.

Apart from the diversity of its inhabitants, what made the concentration camps so revealing from a scientific perspective was the narrow range of possible outcomes. In ordinary life, Levi says, it rarely happens that a man loses himself. We're never alone; our lives are tied to the destinies of our neighbours; it would be exceptional for anyone to achieve unlimited power or fall into utter ruin. Usually we're in possession of at least minimal resources, so the probability of 'total inadequacy' will be small. The final cushion is the law, which in a civilized society will prevent the weak man from becoming too weak and the powerful from becoming too powerful.

In the concentration camp, all that changes. 'Here,' says Levi, 'the struggle to survive is without respite, because everyone is desperately and ferociously alone.' If you vacillate, no one lends a hand; the weak bring benefit to no one. Those who find better ways to survive become stronger and are feared; the rest are knocked aside.

The word they had for the weak, the inept, and the men in decay was 'Muselmann'. The Muselmänner were the 'drowned'. It was the easiest of matters to sink: all that was necessary was to simply carry out orders, eat only the rations, and observe the discipline of the work and camp. It would be exceptional to survive more than three months taking this approach. All of the Muselmänner who were defeated by the camps 'have the same story, or more exactly, have no story; they followed the slope down to the bottom, like streams that run down to the sea'. In their passivity they were overcome before they could adapt. For the Muselmänner, the path to perdition, as Levi puts it, was 'single and broad'.

How was one to avoid becoming a Muselmann?

The paths were many, thought Levi. Some chose the dark route of camp officialdom: these became the directors, the superintendents, the night-guards, and hut-sweepers. These were the *prominenten* who had exchanged solidarity with their comrades for camp privilege. Then there were the true oddballs who would have been unsuited for life outside the camps but by reason of insanity, robust constitutions, or cunning were strangely suited for life within them.

There were also the likes of Alfred L. Alfred L.

had a strategy for getting through the camps. 'L. had a "line": with his hands and face always perfectly clean, he had the rare self-denial to wash his shirt every fortnight, without waiting for the bi-monthly change.' That was harder than it sounds: to wash a shirt in the camps meant finding soap, time, and space in the washroom, keeping watch on the wet shirt without losing attention for a moment, and putting it on again still damp. 'He owned a pair of wooden shoes to go to the shower, and even his striped suit was singularly adapted to his appearance, clean and new.' Shirts, suit, wooden shoes – all this had to be paid for somehow. Alfred L. did it all with bread from his rations.

By taking a course directly opposite to that of the drowned – by asserting and projecting the dignity of his inner nature irrespective of the adversity of the surrounding conditions – he would survive the war.

What the survivor (the 'saved') had over the Muselmann (the 'drowned') was the cultivation of a resilient, productive, and self-aware inner state. The Muselmänner allowed themselves to be defined by their circumstances: they carried out their orders, ate only their rations, and observed the discipline of the work and the camp. The survivors, on the other hand, were able to preserve the coherence of their subjective reality in the face of external shock.

The story of Alfred L. echoes the other accounts of human overcoming that we have considered in this chapter. In each case what we have seen is the

39

triumph of subjective mind over objective conditions. We've seen that excellence in sports is characterized by heightened perception for features of the environment. We've seen the impregnable frame of top sportspeople and some of the techniques that have been employed to create and sustain it. We've seen how frame collapses. And we've seen finally how the same principle may have underpinned the resilience of prisoners in war.

The great spiritual traditions call us repeatedly back to the principle that the inner governs the outer and that what we think and what we say determines how we act and whether we thrive. What we show here is that you don't need to be religious to recognize the substance of this principle. In the eyes of believers the divine calls upon us to pay attention to our inner lights. But our own wellbeing makes exactly the same call.

Answering that call is the first and most important component of generativity.

2

REGULATION OF ENERGY

THE FOX AND THE LION

In his powerful and provocative short book, *The Marriage of Heaven and Hell* (engraved circa 1790), the iconoclastic English poet and artist William Blake confronts the question of energy head-on.

Here, through page after colourful page, Blake in imitation of biblical prophecy expands upon the true nature of humanity and the progression of the contrary universal forces of reason (heaven) and energy (hell). What quickly becomes apparent to the reader is that Blake has a very unusual idea of the relationship between heaven and hell, God and Satan, and angels and devils. For Blake, the former stand for the forces of reason and control; the latter, for irrepressible energy and joy. Here is no good and

41

bad but a play of opposites, each of which reflects one aspect of the divine power.

Blake gives us the Devil's account from the outset. All sacred codes, says Blake's Devil, have been the cause of several errors: first, that man has two real, existing principles – body and soul; second, that energy (called evil) is from body alone and reason (called good) is from soul alone; and third, that God will torment man in eternity for following his energies. That's all wrong, says Blake's Devil. In fact, he says, the contraries are true: man has no body distinct from his soul, for body is 'a portion of soul discerned by the five Senses'; energy is the only life and is from the body, and reason is its outward circumference; and finally, energy is 'eternal delight'.

Blake gathers what he calls 'Proverbs of Hell', and these proverbs are the heart of the work. They are vivid, dynamic, and enigmatic. They talk to us from a world beyond that of our mundane activity and concerns. That's their attraction and their force. Yet for all their strangeness, they revert time and again to the themes of energy and restraint. *Drive your cart and plow over the bones of the dead* – tradition must take second place to productive energy. *Prudence is a rich ugly old maid courted by Incapacity* – the incompetent always want to play safe; but this is unattractive and sterile, and without hope of bringing anything new into the world. *He who desires but acts not, breeds pestilence* – it's unhealthy to harbor desires that are never acted upon. *Prisons are built with stones of Law,*

42

Brothels with bricks of Religion – it's not just that the authorities punish criminality and prostitution; in fact, through their oppressive need for control, they create that very criminality and prostitution in the first place.

Finally: *The fox provides for himself, but God provides for the lion.* This one is more puzzling, but the answer may be this. The fox is the cautious, thoughtful, cunning animal: he can provide for himself. The lion, on the other hand, represents not thoughtfulness but raw energy. As such, it draws upon deep unfathomable power; it does not need to concern itself with pragmatism and calculation.

When it is being itself, it is exactly what it needs to be.

―――――

This chapter is all about energy. It's about how great creative works are born of the uninhibited generation of multiple ideas, the fittest of which survive to become the finished work. It's also about the inner reservoir of energy upon which we draw to get things done – and the ways in which we can run up against its limits. Finally, it's about how that energy is best marshaled as a source of human generativity and what we can do to make it work for us.

DARWINIAN CREATIVITY AND PICASSO'S GUERNICA

Clues as to this aspect of the mystery of generativity can be found embedded in what is arguably the greatest work of art of the twentieth century – Picasso's *Guernica*.[1]

The story behind the mural is well known. It's 1937 and Spain is ravaged by brutal civil war between fascists and republicans. Then – on 26 April 1937 – the German Luftwaffe swoops down upon the small Basque hamlet of Guernica in northern Spain. For three hours the town is pounded by high-explosive and incendiary bombs. The village burns for three days and sixteen hundred civilians are killed or wounded.

The Luftwaffe had, it is said, chosen the town for bombing practice.

Picasso is in Paris at the time, preparing to paint a centerpiece for the Spanish Pavilion of the 1937 World Fair. When the news hits, over a million protesters flood onto the streets in the largest May Day demonstration the capital has ever seen. The news and the images fill the papers. Picasso rushes through the crowds back to his studio and begins sketching. Three months later the giant mural – it's more than eleven feet tall and twenty-five feet wide – is delivered to the Spanish Pavilion.[2]

Often we don't really know how creative acts

come about; generally we only have the finished product and perhaps some words of the creator. *Guernica* is exceptional. Picasso began the work with a series of sketches aimed at depicting the true horror of the bombing. What makes the sketches a truly invaluable resource is that they were consecutively numbered and sometimes individually dated. Rather than just looking at the work as a whole, you can look at the 'bull', say, or the 'horse' or the 'mother with dead child' – all identifiable elements of the completed work – and see how they evolved in the period preceding the completion of the work. It's not quite the same thing as seeing into Picasso's mind, but it's as close as we can realistically get.

The question that Dean Keith Simonton – who carried out the research on *Guernica* – wanted answered was this: did each new sketch represent further progress towards the final work – or did the process show 'blind variation' in the sense that the artist would sometimes pursue ideas that took him nowhere and only after taking some wrong turns decide upon the final composition? Simonton knew he could find out by looking at the relationship between the sketch order and the progress made. If Picasso's progress matched the sketch order, then his creative process would be 'monotonic', meaning that each sketch builds upon the previous sketch and represents a steady advance towards the final composition. If, on the other hand, his progress does not increase steadily with the sketch order –

if sometimes Picasso makes progress but sometimes he heads down a blind alley – then the process could be said to have been 'non-monotonic'.

Here's what Simonton saw when he plotted progress score[3] against sketch order:[4]

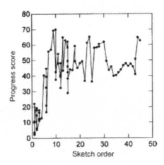

Figure 2. *Plot of estimated progress scores as a function of true sketch order. Vertical lines connect figures that came from the same sketch (e.g., compositional groups).*

This is precisely what would be expected if Picasso's creative process was *non*-monotonic. You can see that Picasso is making erratic progress for the first few sketches. Then from sketches five through ten he makes tremendous progress, to the extent that the tenth sketch is as close to his final masterpiece as it will ever be. The remaining thirty-five sketches show steps forward and steps back as Picasso explores various possibilities and assesses whether or not they will contribute to his final composition.

Simonton then decided to repeat the analysis for those sketches that contained only a single figure.

46

Let's take the 'horse' and the 'mother with dead child' as examples. Here are Simonton's graphs:[5]

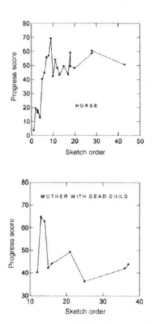

What you see for the horse is broadly similar to what you see for the sketches as a whole: Picasso makes the most significant progress between sketches five and ten; after sketch ten there are steps forward and steps back as he explores various possibilities. Now look at the graph for the 'mother with dead child'. In this case Picasso also makes most of his progress in the earlier sketches. What's more obvious than with the horse is that it's a *very* early sketch that shows most progress towards the final version – none of the later

47

sketches even come close. Picasso gets it more or less right early on in the process. Then he experiments with other possibilities to see how they will turn out – and finally settles for his early version after all.

What all this shows, according to Simonton, is that the creative process is 'Darwinian'. What he means by this is that the creator doesn't set out with a specific destination and then take sure and steady steps towards it. Nor is there a single eureka moment when it all falls into place. Instead, the creator engages in a trial-and-error process that produces more ideas than will ever be used and then selects the best from among them. It's akin to Darwinian theory in that the creative process throws up a whole bunch of variants and the stronger variants 'survive', so to speak, in the final work.

Put the theory to one side and begin to imagine what it would have actually felt like to be Picasso working on *Guernica*. It's one thing to struggle onwards, even making only small steps forward from a modest starting point, if each step improves upon the last. But Simonton's graphs show that at many points in the process Picasso's efforts did not take him forward. They took him *backwards*. That's another thing altogether. What must he have thought and felt when he reached sketch thirty-five and saw his work no closer to the final version than he had been at sketch ten? And yet we can't possibly say that Picasso was doing anything wrong – the final works vindicate him on that front. The better approach is to recognize and accept that progress is made not by seeking perfection, but by permitting the perfect to emerge from a mass of imperfect items.

This all confirms what has been said of Picasso elsewhere. 'Faced with an empty canvas or a blank sheet of paper he does not think things out: he makes a start and lets his picture lead him on, knowing that he will begin all over again if he is not satisfied. Which explains how he could once say to Vlamnick, in the days when they were friends: "How on earth did I manage to do that?"'[6] Picasso is the most prolific artist in history – he produced an astounding 147,800 works of art, or an average of around 1,780 pieces per year over his eighty-three or so years of creativity.

How generalizable is this? If the top producers in art, music, literature, and even entrepreneurship achieve what they do through a trial-and-error process like this, then there's something important we can learn from it. What generativity requires, in this view, is for the process of creation to be bold and uninhibited. We don't pre-select our own brilliant products; we let them emerge in their varied forms and in their own way. Many of the early ideas won't make it through to the final cut; but many of the later ideas won't make it either, and it may sometimes prove to be the case that what came out first, came out best.

INNER RESOURCE

What Darwinian creativity shows is that in creative work it is the unhindered generation of ideas that is primary – and that the critical processes of self-assessment and selection ('survival of the fittest') happen later. Does it really follow, though, that our enterprises are generally – and across multiple fields of human endeavour – best carried out freely and without inhibition?

———

An answer to this may be found in the concept of 'inner resource'.

———

Inner resource can be considered the store of energy we draw upon to self-regulate. When we resist temptation, exercise choice and responsibility, or suppress thoughts or emotions, we draw upon this store of energy. It's a single store that is relied upon to do all these things; and it's a store that can be depleted from overuse, leaving us less able to self-regulate ourselves later on. This means not just impairment to self-control, but also impairments to performance and persistence.

This is a radically new idea. Historically we have

tended to think of self-control rather differently. Probably the most common view is that self-control is a kind of *skill*. In this view, we gradually develop the skill of self-control over long periods of time. A related approach is to view self-control as a kind of *knowledge*, such that we know or can learn how to alter our own responses or states. Either way, once developed and sufficiently practiced, we don't expect any sudden drop-offs. We know how to manage ourselves and maintain our poise and bearing.

Here's what the science tells us: that resisting desire, exercising choice, restraining emotion, and suppressing thoughts *all* lead to impaired performance on other tasks that require self-regulation.

Imagine, for example, being taken into a room in which chocolate chip cookies had just been baked and laid out upon a table. The air is filled with the aroma of the fresh chocolate and baking. You've been told to skip a meal and you are famished. Other people are allowed to tuck in merrily to the cookies and chocolates. You, however, are instructed to snack only on a bowl of red and white radishes. After this, you're asked to carry out a geometric puzzle. (The puzzle is insoluble – but you're not told that.) You might be surprised to find that you would tend to give up rather easily – in fact, you would be likely to give up, on average, more than twice as quickly as the cookie-eaters, and you would make only around half as many attempts.

Now imagine watching a tear-jerking movie while being required to neither show nor feel any emotion. Afterwards you are asked to unscramble a series of anagrams. The results are no less surprising. You would, on average, solve the problems almost 50 percent more effectively if you had been allowed to let your emotions flow, without any effort to deny or hide them, while watching the film.[7]

Suppressing thoughts leads to similar performance decrements. In the tests that have been done, people give up much more quickly after repressing thoughts than when either expressing those thoughts or with no thought control at all.[8] Suppressing thoughts seems to expend the same energy that we have to use to persist in activities – and has a predictably negative effect on outcomes.

Finally, the same kind of impairment occurs not only after exercising self-restraint but also after making choices, as has been shown by Kathleen Vohs of the University of Minnesota. Vohs conducted a total of seven experiments involving almost four hundred subjects both inside the laboratory and out on the streets and malls of the United States. Some of the participants were asked to make choices about consumer products, university courses, and study materials. Others were not asked to make choices, but

52

simply to consider the options in front of them. They were then asked to carry out various unpleasant or challenging tasks: for example, participants were asked to hold their arms in ice water, or drink diluted vinegar, or solve mathematical problems.

People who had been required to make choices were, Vohs found, considerably worse at maintaining focus when trying to solve problems or complete an unpleasant task. The strength of the effect is illustrated by what is known as the 'cold pressor' challenge, which requires participants to hold their arms in ice water. Those who had not made choices beforehand did reasonably well on the challenge – tolerating an average of sixty-seven seconds of intense cold. Those who *had* made choices prior to dunking their arms in the freezing water, on the other hand, were unable to hold out, averaging a measly twenty-eight seconds. In the words of Vohs, they suffered from 'decision fatigue' or 'cognitive depletion'.[9] In other words, they had less of that inner energy you need to focus and overcome difficulty.

What is especially striking about the last point is that these detrimental effects occur even when we make choices freely and in accordance with our wishes and attitudes. For example, when making a choice between two diametrically opposed courses of action, it didn't matter which was chosen – it was the mere fact of having to choose at all that caused the detriment.

All decision-makers – not just creatives – benefit from awareness of what happens when we deplete the inner energy we use to self-regulate. That's because decision making itself, as we have seen, both relies upon and depletes this self-regulatory resource.

When judges decide whether or not to grant parole, for example, it is decision fatigue that appears to have the greatest impact.[10] The effect is dramatic and disconcerting: the percentage of favourable rulings drops from around 65 percent to nearly zero within each decision session and returns abruptly to nearly 65 percent after a break. The graph below[11] shows the proportion of rulings in favour of prisoners (y axis) against the order in which the decisions were made (x axis), with circles representing the first decision in three decision sessions and dotted lines representing a food break. Over a thousand rulings of eight judges were recorded over a ten-month period. While decision fatigue can substantially reduce the chance of a favourable decision, it is curious that legally relevant considerations – severity of the crime and prison time served – exerted no effect on the rulings.

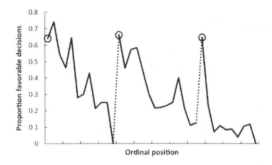

A prisoner whose case comes up first thing in the morning, then, has a good chance of convincing the judge that he is worthy of consideration for parole. As the morning wears on, the chance goes down. The prisoner who appears immediately after the morning break, however, also has a good chance of obtaining a favourable ruling, which again drops and continues dropping for prisoners appearing later on. The difference in outcomes is striking. A prisoner whose case comes up before lunch has a near zero probability of release; one whose case comes up immediately after lunch, on the other hand, has around a 65 percent chance of being granted parole.

The researchers attribute the effect to mental depletion. What happens is that the judges find rejecting requests to be the safest and easiest decision: this effectively preserves the status quo and is associated with shorter decision time and shorter written decisions. It is therefore the likelier outcome when judges are mentally depleted as a result of the number of previous decisions they have had to make.

Decision making can be impaired on many fronts. Compromise and integrative thinking are reduced, and simplistic decisions take their place. Decision-makers will be more inclined to choose the 'standard' response or the response that preserves the status quo. Decisions are increasingly likely to be based on irrelevant information. They may also be postponed or avoided altogether.[12] People's IQ scores drop as does their performance on other tests of logic.[13]

What really is this resource? It's been said by the researchers that although they can infer the existence of the resource, they don't have a clear understanding of its nature. But we can draw some conclusions.

It's important. Choice, responsibility, and self-control are all-pervading features of human life. These matters are so fundamental that it's hard to imagine an activity or enterprise in which the resource isn't engaged – and routinely engaged at that.

It's surprisingly limited. A mere five-minute exercise in resisting the temptation to eat cookies and chocolate resulted in a doubling of the time taken by people to solve puzzles.

And it's counterintuitive. Of course, it's not hard to understand and accept how exercising self-control could have detrimental effects: it can be tiring and irritating to have to say 'no'. But this same resource was also impaired by suppressing thoughts or by merely making choices – even choices that are freely made and in accordance with our underlying attitudes and values. The resource is engaged and depleted by a wide range of acts that draw upon the exercise of will or volition.

It has been said that the resource is, in fact, like a muscle. We have only a limited capacity to control and alter behavior, and this capacity appears to be vulnerable to depletion after serious use. When we have experienced intense demands for self-control, or when we squander self-control in unproductive activity, we may find ourselves in a situation where self-control breaks down in other, unrelated spheres.[14]

How to self-control without self-control, so to speak? Is there a way to square the circle? Possibly, yes. The focus here has been on *construal*: the way in which people subjectively construe a situation, an object, or a desire. Related to this is the focus on what psychologists call 'cognitive transformations'. Cognitive transformation is all about sense making – or, here, making sense of experience in a way that has not been done before.

At its simplest, this may just mean thinking about

something differently. One of the ways that the transformation can be effected, for example, is to switch from thinking in a consummatory to a non-consummatory manner. If we think in a consummatory way, we're usually thinking about satisfying our drives: for example, thinking about how a marshmallow would melt sweetly on the tongue. But it is always open to reconceive of the marshmallow: to imagine it from a purely visual or aesthetic standpoint. It's the same marshmallow we're thinking about, but in an entirely different light. It has been cognitively transformed.

It can also mean thinking about something on a different level entirely. A distinguishing feature between mental construals, for example, is level of abstraction. It is possible to shift thinking on any particular occasion to a higher level of abstraction: this allows us to capture the general meaning of an event by reference to broad class of examples. It is equally possible to shift thinking down to a lower level of abstraction, enabling us to think about the concrete features that render events unique. We can shift to a higher, more abstract level by asking 'why-type' questions (why do you like this?) or by categorizing objects and events (a dog is a canine); we can shift to a lower, more concrete level by asking 'how-type' questions (how do you do this?) or by finding exemplars of general categories (a small black poodle is a kind of dog).

In each case, the effects can be profound. The

evidence shows that when we are thinking about chocolate in odd or novel ways, for example, we actually like it less and find it less tasty than if we think about its sensory aspects. When we are able to shift our thinking to a higher, more abstract level, similar results are obtained: thinking abstractly, we prefer and are far more likely to choose, if offered, an apple over a candy bar. What is striking is that all that is required to do this is to categorize – to think about on a more abstract plane – a series of items that may be totally unrelated to health or dieting. There is something in the very act of shifting our thought to this higher, more abstract level that empowers self-control, irrespective of its particular context.[15]

───

Successful creators often have the most idiosyncratic – one might say indulgent – rituals. Hemingway wrote standing up. Ben Franklin wrote in the bathtub. Balzac ate a big meal at five in the evening, slept until midnight, then got up to write at a small desk in his room for sixteen hours, drinking endless cups of coffee. 'Schiller kept rotten apples in the desk; Shelley and Rousseau remained bareheaded in the sunshine; Boussuet worked in a cold room with his head wrapped in furs; Grétry and Schiller immersed their feet in ice-cold water; . . . Guido Reni could paint, and de Musset could write poetry, only when dressed in magnificent style; . . . The aesthetician, Baumgarten, advised poets seeking inspiration to ride on horseback, to drink wine in moderation, and provided they were chaste, to look at beautiful women.'[16]

Yet creators are also notable for discipline and regimentation. Marcel Proust worked in absolute silence. Toni Morrison wrote in a motel room; E. B. White in a cabin by the shore.[17] B. F. Skinner, the great behaviouralist psychologist, wrote *Schedules of Reinforcement* with C. B. Ferster in a room dedicated to writing. They wrote between 9 am and lunchtime only – and would not work in the afternoon even if they wanted to. There would be no visitors, no phone calls, no warm up or inactive periods, and no private conversations.[18]

This chapter has suggested that the apparent contradiction between idiosyncratic self-indulgence and monkish self-restraint may in fact be no true contradiction at all. In each case, the creator ensures that energy is preserved for the creative task, in the first case by reducing unnecessary self-restraint and in the latter case by eliminating unnecessary distraction. Each creator adopts the particular course that serves his or her purposes best.

Let's look once again at Picasso, only this time from the perspective of a full lifetime.

Well before *Guernica*, Picasso had learned how to cultivate a habit that was maximally effective for him. In his early years, during what was called his blue period, he entered into a relationship with Fernande Olivier, a lady who has been described as 'a passive, sensual creature, a true harem flower'. They lived together, short of cash, in the rundown Parisian tenement and haven for bohemian artists known as the Bateau-Lavoir. This was a time of terrible poverty for the struggling artist and his young lover. On winter days when they had no coal left for the stove, they would huddle together in bed; at other times they would live off the food that had been left at their door by anonymous well-wishers.

Yet this was also leading to a period of tremendous creativity – so much so that Gertrude Stein called the number of pictures painted from 1904 to 1906 'incredible'. And it was also the period in which Picasso laid down his basic working system. In broad terms it was simple – the night for painting, and the day for sleep and pleasure:

> He had chosen this curious division of time because at night he could be sure of working in peace. Thus he painted by the light of his big oil lamp and went to bed only at dawn. At four in the afternoon he got up, had his breakfast, took a bath – the water for his tub had been heating on the stove – and then received

his friends in the studio, or, on fine days, on the square
which served as a common room for the tenants of
the Bateau. In the evening he generally went out for
dinner with them. ... At ten o'clock at night, whatever
the company, he would get up from table and go home
to start work. His friends were used to his timetable
and respected his sleep in the morning, leaving
strangers who came and woke him up to suffer the
onslaught of his fury.

And some fury it was: when several German artists
came up to tell Picasso how much they admired him,
they were greeted with revolver shots and hurried
back over the Seine without knowing what had
happened to them.[19]

Picasso didn't just organize his periods of work
and rest over the course of a day – he also did this
over the course of his lifetime, and to great effect.
Prior to the next great period of creativity, Picasso
took himself away from Paris back to a place of total
seclusion. The particular location he chose was the
remote little village of Gosol, in the Spanish Pyrenees
close to the Andorra valley, which is over four
thousand feet above sea level and could only be
reached by mule or on foot. In a long summer stay,
Picasso did a great deal of work, drawing peasants and
filling notebooks with sketches, the primitive setting
inspiring a new, simplified style. It was the beginning
of his Cubist period of multi-view figures and natural
forms presented in geometric states, which would

give rise, most famously, to *Les Demoiselles d'Avignon* in 1907. The stimulus to his creative flow was so dramatic that he finished the portrait of Gertrude Stein – which hitherto had he had worked at in vain in over eighty sittings – in a few sessions in the new style. Only Stein was unimpressed: 'It doesn't look like me!' she exclaimed. 'You'll see,' replied Picasso. 'One day you'll end up looking like your portrait.' And that (as his biographer says) is what happened.[20]

Where Picasso was really able to channel his energies was in his capacity to bring his life into his art. While it is widely known that his life falls into several phases, it is less well known that 'each new epoch blossoms with paintings of a new woman – not a sitter or a model, but a mistress – each of whom is touted to have served Picasso as an incandescent, albeit temporary, muse'.[21] For the Rose Period there is Fernande Olivier, for Cubism comes Eva Gouel, for his post-war neoclassicism comes Olga Khokhlova, and for surrealism, Marie-Therese Walter. Picasso painted each of them in his characteristic style of the period, merging and harmonizing artistic and personal interests to the fullest extent. Another of his lovers, Dora Maar, was depicted at once full-face and in profile, with lopsided features and asymmetric eyes. When asked how he could deal so harshly with a beautiful face, he could only answer: 'For me, she is the weeping woman. For years I gave her a tortured appearance, not out of sadism, and without any pleasure on my part, but in obedience to a vision that had imposed itself on me.'[22] Dora Maar can in fact be seen in the screaming, weeping woman holding a dead child in *Guernica*.

Picasso was the arch self-regulator. He shows what can be achieved not just by adapting rhythms of life so as to be minimally depleting, but also by channeling his interests and inclinations into his work. This is definitively not just a question of 'letting go'. It is a careful marshaling of desires and drives and making them the underpinning of one's mission. Picasso wasn't productive simply because he did what he wanted – he was productive because he knew how to find what he wanted in what he was actually doing.

If a resource is valuable and limited, then one obvious conclusion is that it should be employed selectively and not frittered away. It should be called upon with prudence and saved for when it is most needed.

We need, one might say, to 'get monkish' – to eliminate distractions or reduce them to a minimum. Modern life requires incessant self-regulation and choice making, from simply dealing with traffic to navigating the many potential *faux pas* of the workplace. Whereas hitherto we may have prided ourselves on our hard-earned skills in keeping ourselves well organized and controlled, it may be that all this time we have been making costly withdrawals on a limited supply of energy. The more we can do to keep those withdrawals light and sparse, the better.

On the other hand, insofar as to get things done we sometimes do need to battle against ourselves, those battles need to be picked – and timed – carefully. Let go and indulge when it can be done without harm. We should recognize that at those moments when we need to be at peak performance, we shouldn't be trying to score little victories of self-control against ourselves.

And at the deepest level, we need to reflect and turn in upon ourselves to find out what psychological 'trash' we are carrying around that itself is bearing upon our limited energy and sapping it away for no good reason. Racial bias, for example, has been shown to draw on this same resource, causing reductions in cognitive performance.[23] Why burden ourselves with that – to our own detriment?

———

Modern science cannot take sole credit for recognizing the perils of an errant mind. One of Buddhism's greatest teachings, for example, is that a man is not his thoughts and feelings, nor a woman hers. The true self is the quiet watcher of all these swirls and eddies of the mind. Clarity can be established when the true self is able to detach itself from the contents of the mind and observe them dispassionately, whereas confusion occurs when the true self confuses itself with these mental contents. Buddhism provides practical methods of dealing with these problems – mindfulness and the stilling of thoughts – that are both elegant and time-tested.[24]

Where the Buddhist texts speak of mindfulness and stilling of thoughts, the contemporary psychological research speaks of self-regulation and cognitive transformation. Nevertheless, the similarity between the ancient wisdom and modern science is striking. Both recognize and communicate the following as basic truths: that the exercise of self-control is not an easy or trouble-free process; that energy is thus consumed; and there are better and more sophisticated ways than simply making the effort of holding back.

Both the ancient wisdom and modern science tend, in fact, to offer the same fundamental guidance. That is this: the road to enlightened self-regulation or self-control comes through the mind acting on the mind, not to repress – but to re-imagine, reinterpret, and reframe. It is to grasp that the way the mind works is not fixed; that we can choose the way we construe objects and events; and that this is the path to the kind of freedom that really matters.

SOCIAL
INFLUENCE

WHAT AMERICAN GOTHIC *TELLS US*

Consider the image below.

This is, of course, Grant Wood's *American Gothic*.[1] The painting, which was first exhibited in 1930 at The Art Institute of Chicago, brought Wood instant recognition. It has since gone on to become a foundation stone of the American self-imagination. Even today, critics debate whether it was intended as a satire at the expense of the repression and priggishness of middle America – something that Wood denied – or whether it was meant as a tribute to the simple moral virtues of rural people.

What concerns us at the moment, though, is one aspect of *American Gothic* in particular. What Wood has managed to capture so superbly is the way that the faces of this couple – who have, no doubt, lived together as husband and wife for a quarter of a century or more – have converged. The man is obviously somewhat older than the woman; his eyes are shadowed and his skin bears the marks of the years. Apart from that, their faces are eerily similar. Their equally large, domed foreheads dominate the picture; each gazes out unblinkingly, with eyes wide open and only the barest traces of eyelids. Both have thin, puckered lips; both hold their heads stiffly erect. They could almost be brother and sister. And that may be why the painting is so haunting to some people – it holds the remote and unpalatable possibility of incest and inbreeding.

———

There is, however, good reason to think that the phenomenon of facial convergence has another (and altogether more wholesome) origin, in what psychologists call 'the chameleon effect'. The chameleon effect refers to the reflex mimicry of gestures, postures, and facial expressions of other people with whom we are interacting. Just as chameleons adapt the colour of their skin to match the colour of the environment they are in, so we adapt our expressions and gestures to match those of whomever we happen to be interacting with. What is more, psychologists now believe that this is an automatic reaction. If the person you are interacting with smiles, you will be more likely to smile in return. If they rub their face, you will be more likely to rub your face. If they wiggle their foot, you will be that much more likely to wiggle your foot too. And none of this depends on any conscious strategy to ingratiate yourself or curry favour. It will just happen.

That's why the faces of partners come to resemble each other over the years, according to the psychologist Robert Zajonc and his colleagues. Zajonc got hold of photographs of couples in their first year of marriage and again after twenty-five years of married life. He cropped the photos and had any extraneous non-facial material removed. The photographs were then shown to a test group of over one hundred participants, who were asked to indicate how similar the faces appeared and what they thought the likelihood was that the individuals depicted were married to each other. The results showed that couples became more similar facially after twenty-five years of marriage. The researchers ruled out the possibility of environmental factors (e.g., climate or socioeconomic position) causing the difference by taking all their couples from the same part of the American Midwest and ensuring that they were matched on other socioeconomic variables. They then ruled out the possibility of diet causing the similarity by means of an additional study. In the end they concluded that the most likely explanation was that couples had been mimicking each other's facial expressions, with the effect that repeated imitation over the years had left similar facial lines – the chameleon effect.[2]

WHY FAT FRIENDS MAKE YOU FAT

The profound effects that our social contacts can have on our general wellbeing have been forcefully illustrated in research from Harvard Medical School on the causes of obesity.[3] It's well known, of course, that obesity has been on the rise over the course of the last several decades – in the United States alone, for example, the prevalence of obesity has risen from 23 percent to 33 percent in recent years, and fully 66 percent of adults are overweight. This is commonly attributed to poor diet and lack of exercise – which no doubt have their part to play. But this can only be part of the answer, because poor diet and lack of exercise are also choices, and there must also be reasons why people make those choices.

Is there something in a person's social contacts that might make them more susceptible to obesity?

The research evaluated a network of more than twelve thousand people who underwent repeated measurements over a period of thirty-two years. It focused on clusters of obese persons within the network and looked at the association between the weight gain of individuals and the weight gain among that individual's social contacts. It also examined the dependence of that association on the nature of the social ties involved – friendship, sibling, marital, etc. – as well as gender and geographic distance.

If you had been one of those 12,067 individuals included in the study, you would no doubt have been shocked by the degree to which your physical shape is determined merely by your social contacts. In all of the examinations, from 1971 to 2003, the risk of your becoming obese would have increased by 45 percent if you were connected to another obese person in the network by one degree of separation – if you had an obese friend, for instance, or your partner or sibling was obese. Even more surprising would be the fact that your chance of becoming obese would increase even at two or three degrees of separation – at two degrees of separation, the risk increased by about 20 percent, and at three degrees of separation by about 10 percent. Your odds of becoming obese would increase even if the only obese person you knew was your partner's brother, or (even more remotely) your sister's husband's best friend.

Admittedly, there was some variation in the results. In general, those with obese friends were 57 percent more likely to become obese themselves, but this includes friendships reported by one partner only (i.e., non-mutual friendships); when the friendship is truly mutual, the increased likelihood of obesity shoots up to 171 percent. The phenomenon is, additionally, more likely to occur among same-sex friends, and most likely of all to occur among same-sex *male* friends. You would be 40 percent more likely to become obese if your sibling became obese, and you would be 37 percent more likely to become obese if your spouse became obese. Smoking and geographic distance (as opposed to social distance) made no difference.

The burning question is: why? Are we seeing here the chameleon effect 'writ large' – unconscious imitation of behaviour, much like husband and wife over many decades unconsciously imitate each other's facial expressions? The difficulty, of course, is that the 'contagion' of obesity is unaffected by geographical distance; it is *social distance* that matters. More likely, then, that contagion takes place through the shifting of norms about the acceptability of being overweight. We observe changes in those around us and tend to accept those changes occurring to ourselves. Imperceptibly, we gain weight.

THE MAKING OF SCIENTISTS

It is obvious that this phenomenon could provide answers to the question: what goes into the making of eminent individuals across the various fields of human achievement?

———

Let's start with an eminent individual from the scientific field – Sir Hans Krebs. Krebs was a German-born British physician and biochemist who won the Nobel Prize in Physiology or Medicine in 1953 for his discovery of the citric acid cycle (now often eponymously known as the 'Krebs cycle'). The citric acid cycle forms the very basis for life: it describes a series of chemical reactions used by all aerobic organisms to generate energy from food. At the outset of his career Krebs studied medicine and chemistry in Gottingen, Hamburg, and Berlin, before working in roles as a research assistant and in hospital. When the National Socialist Party came to power in Germany, Krebs was removed from his position and went to England, where he occupied a series of academic roles in Cambridge and elsewhere.

After being awarded the Nobel Prize, Krebs had – perhaps unsurprisingly – asked himself how it had happened.[4] Here's how he put it. On the day he found himself in Stockholm, he said, he realized that he owed his good fortune to the fact that at the critical stage of his academic career – between the ages of 25 and 29 – he was associated with Otto Warburg in Berlin. It was Otto Warburg who had set an example of the methods and quality of first-rate research, and without that example Krebs would never have reached the standards required by the Nobel Committees.

Otto Warburg (1883-1970) was himself a Nobel laureate who had received the prize in 1931 for his work on the enzyme in the reactions between oxygen and foodstuffs in cellular respiration. Interestingly, Warburg had asked himself the same question as Krebs had asked: what was the turning point on his road towards achievement? His answer is recorded in an autobiographical note. The most important event in the professional development of a young scientist, said Warburg, is 'personal contact with the great scientists of his time'. In Warburg's case, the turning point came when he was accepted in 1903 by the chemist Emil Fischer as a co-worker in protein chemistry. For three years Warburg met Fischer almost daily to work under his guidance.

So here we have the beginning of a lineage running back from Krebs directly to Warburg, and from Warburg directly to Fischer.

Emil Fischer (1852-1919), Warburg's mentor, has been called 'one of the most outstanding chemists of his time'. He was awarded a Nobel Prize in 1902 for work on the chemical structure of sugars. Fischer was a pupil and associate of Adolf von Baeyer, who received the Nobel Prize for discoveries in the field of chemistry of dyestuffs. Von Baeyer (1835-1917) was a pupil of Kekulé (who was renowned for his work on the structure of organic compounds, especially the ring structure of benzene), and Kekulé (1829-1896) was a pupil of Liebig, who is considered the founder of organic chemistry. As the first Nobel Prize was only awarded in 1901, neither Kekulé nor Liebig (1803-1873) could possibly have attained one; had the Nobel existed in their time, 'they would certainly have been laureates'.[5]

And it doesn't even stop there. Liebig was a pupil of the French chemist Gay-Lussac, who had discovered some of the fundamental laws of the behaviour of gases. Gay-Lussac (1778-1850) had himself developed from the French school of chemists associated in particular with Berthollet. Berthollet (1748-1822) was a pioneer of combustion and the role of oxygen in that process. Bethollet was himself taught by Lavoisier. Lavoisier (1743-1794) named the elements carbon, hydrogen, and oxygen.

Arranged schematically, the scientific lineage stretching from Lavoisier and Berthollet in the eighteenth century to Krebs in the twentieth century looks like this:

Berthollet 1748-1822
↓
Gay-Lussac 1778-1850
↓
Liebig 1803-1873
↓
Kekulé 1829-1896
↓
von Baeyer 1835-1917
↓
Fischer 1852-1919
↓
Warburg 1883-1970
↓
Krebs 1900-1981

What we have now is a direct, unbroken chain showing the lineage of great scientists from as far back as the eighteenth century – from Berthollet to Gay-Lussac, then to Liebig, to Kekulé, to von Baeyer, to Fischer, to Warburg and finally through to Krebs himself. In addition to the unbroken nature of the chain, what also stands out is the reiteration of the basic theme of indebtedness to a mentor. Even five scientific 'generations' back in the nineteenth century, Liebig had this to say about his mentor: 'The course of my whole life was determined by the fact that Gay-Lussac accepted me in his laboratory as a collaborator and pupil.' As Krebs himself put it: 'In every case the association between teacher and pupil was close and prolonged, extending to the mature stage of the pupil, to what we would now call postgraduate and doctorate levels. It was not merely a matter of attending a course of lectures but of researching together over a period of years.'[6]

Relax the criteria slightly by allowing for horizontal links among multiple pupils, and the scientific lineage expands into a full-blown family tree. Here's the family tree stemming from just one of the progenitors, von Baeyer:

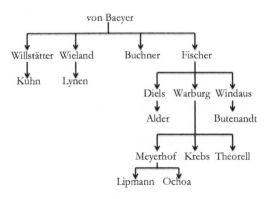

There are seventeen names, all associated with major scientific discoveries.

———

Krebs in his account explains what he individually learned from his own mentor, Otto Warburg. He found in Warburg, he says, an example of asking the right kind of question, of forging new tools for tackling problems, of being ruthless in self-criticism, of being painstaking in verifying facts, of expressing results and ideas clearly and concisely, and of focusing life on true values. Warburg himself had noted of his own mentor, Fischer, that he learned that the scientist had to have the courage to attack the 'great unsolved problems of his time'. Others make similar remarks.

What is evident is that the true basis of the inheritance that is passed down from generation to generation is not knowledge as much as an approach or set of values. Krebs – the ultimate beneficiary of this long line of scientific achievement – was very clear about this. Both knowledge and technical skills, he said, could be learned from many teachers. What was crucial was to learn the *attitudes* of the distinguished teacher: the use of skills, how to assess their potentialities and limitations, and how to rejuvenate and supplement them. Above all was the attitude of humility – since it was from this that came the self-critical mind and the continuous effort to learn and improve.[7]

PSYCHIC ENVIRONMENTS

Humans are not, in this analysis, isolated atomistic units. We are porous and vulnerable to influence both for better and for worse. This includes but isn't necessarily limited to particular individuals. Above and beyond the people with whom we share our lives is what could loosely be called the psychic or mental environment: the sum total of the images, words, and sensations as experienced by an individual human being.

Psychic environments take on a particular importance as a result of what is known as 'ideomotor action'. Ideomotor action occurs when the mere thinking (having a mental 'idea') about a behaviour increases the tendency to engage in that behaviour: we're more likely to dance when we think about dancing, for example, and we're also more likely to yawn when we think about yawning. If that's the case, then there's every reason to think that the process can be set in motion not only by thoughts, but also by perceptions. An idea can be introduced from the outside, which then (like any idea) is liable to increase the likelihood of its corresponding action.

What the research shows is that human behaviours can be activated by the mere presence of environmental features. In one experiment, participants were exposed by way of a scrambled sentence test to a series of words priming the concept 'rude': 'aggressively', 'bold', 'rude', 'bother', 'disturb', 'intrude', 'annoyingly', 'interrupt', 'audaciously', 'brazen', 'impolitely', 'infringe', 'obnoxious', 'aggravating', and 'bluntly'. The aim of the experiment was to find out how rude they had become, merely through unconscious exposure to words, and this was done by measuring how long it would take for them to interrupt a conversation being held between the experimenter and someone else. Those primed in the rude condition interrupted in an average of 326 seconds (or around 5½ minutes) – compared with 9 to 10 minutes on average for those primed in a non-rude condition. In a 10-minute period, those in the rude condition interrupted more than 60 percent of the time, compared with interrupting less than 20 percent of the time for those in the polite prime.

It's not only words that can have this effect. In a similar experiment, participants were primed to an 'elderly' *stereotype* triggered by concepts such as 'old', 'lonely', 'forgetful', 'retired', 'wrinkle', 'bingo', and 'Florida'. After the experiment, those primed using this elderly stereotype actually walked more slowly down a corridor. In another experiment, merely exposing participants to black and white photographs of African Americans for between thirteen and twenty-seven milliseconds increased their hostility level. Those who were low in racist attitudes towards African Americans were just as likely to respond in this way as those high in racist attitudes.[8]

———

There are several points to make about this.

First, what is happening is not the same thing as was once said to happen in the old 'subliminal' advertising. With subliminal advertising, the idea was to flash up frames of Pepsi bottles or popcorn in the middle of a movie to make audiences go and buy soft drinks or popcorn. What is occurring in the modern studies is far more subtle. The primed behaviours of the subjects were already within the range of feasible responses to the situations in which they found themselves; they were already in the 'behavioural repetoire'. Subjects were not being primed to do anything out of the ordinary or anything that they were not already doing. They were, to adapt the modern phrase, being 'nudged' to carry on doing what they were doing but do it differently.

The second thing is that people don't have a clue that it's happening. Participants were debriefed and almost without exception showed no awareness of the effect being tested. In the final experiment, only two participants could see a face, and even they couldn't identify whether it was African American or Caucasian. That has implications for how we deal with the phenomenon when it does occur; as the authors of the study say, we need to be aware of the automatic influence, or at least the possibility of it, before we can control it.

Third, the phenomenon can trigger self-fulfilling effects. When we see something happening in the world outside (aggression, say, or love), we have a tendency to respond to it, automatically, in kind. Of course, the same applies to others: they see us responding in a certain way and have a tendency to respond to that, also automatically, and also in kind. There is an ongoing feedback loop between ourselves and the environment around us, including its people. It's potentially a kind of perpetual motion machine, and it highlights how people affect each other in ways of which they may not be fully conscious.

This doesn't always mean that the effects are always helpful. When well-known exemplars (as opposed to stereotypes) of a particular skill are presented, the effect is to *inhibit* the corresponding behaviour in the observer. When photographs of famous footballers are presented, foot motion is inhibited; when photographs of famous tennis-players are presented, it is hand motion that slows down.[9] When primed by way of a stereotype (e.g., 'professor'), performance in intelligence tests is enhanced. But when presented with 'Albert Einstein' as a specific well-known exemplar, performance in intelligence tests is impaired.[10] It is thought that this occurs due to quick – and negative – automatic comparisons with the well-known figures.

———

Imagine what this means. It means that there is almost nothing that we take in – words or images – that is not able, in some way, to affect the way we are going to behave. The effect may be subtle; it may be more like 'nudging' than pushing. The effect will almost always be invisible. But it's there and it's profound.

———

Contagion is, in fact, not merely a matter of behaviour – it is also a matter of *goals*. Certain actions imply certain kinds of goals, and those goals (and not just the actions by which they are manifested) are themselves contagious. We tend to abstract the goals implied by the behaviour of others and imitate them. What is more, this process is also automatic.

For the sake of illustration, have a brief look at the following scenario (Scenario 1):

Bas is meeting a former college friend called Natasha

while having a beer in his favourite pub. They are having a chat, and Bas tells her about his new job. The atmosphere in the pub is great, and a lot of people have been showing up. At the end of the evening, people start to dance. Bas looks at the dance floor from a distance, and thinks, 'Isn't this a nice place to be?'

It is likely that you have correctly identified that in this scenario Bas is an amiable person having a drink with his old friend Natasha and enjoying the ambience of the pub. Now – having read this scenario – imagine that you are asked to help out a female undergraduate by giving feedback on a computer skills task she had designed. You would probably help her out of kindness, but you might not invest a great deal of time and effort in assisting an unknown undergraduate with her studies.

Now have a look at this scenario (Scenario 2):

Bas is meeting a former college friend called Natasha while having a beer in his favourite pub. They are having a chat, and Bas tells her about his new job. The atmosphere in the pub is great, and a lot of people have been showing up. At the end of the evening, Bas walks Natasha home. When they arrive at her home, he asks her, 'May I come in?'

In this scenario, Bas is doing more than just enjoying a quiet drink and the atmosphere of the bar; he is also opportunistically making the most of his prior acquaintance with Natasha. To put it simply, Bas is acting with clear sexual intent. *Now* imagine that female undergraduate has come to you asking for help with her assignment. Would you help her?

This is precisely the test that was carried out on forty-eight young Dutchmen by Henk Aarts and colleagues at the University of Utrecht. What they found was that the young men were far more likely to help out the (imaginary) undergraduate after reading Scenario 2 than they were after reading Scenario 1. Simply by reading the second short passage about a man walking a woman home and inviting himself in for a drink, the men had (as it were) been infected by his goal of seeking casual sex and were themselves more inclined to help out a woman. The participants were doing much more than imitating Bas' behaviour (which would have been impossible in the circumstances) – they were beginning to imitate the goal that his behaviour implied. This is what is known as 'goal contagion', and it has been shown to work similarly for other goals, such as making money.[11]

THE MAKING OF ARTISTS

It's the contention of the chapter that creativity is a function not only of individuals but also of environments and the people who inhabit them. If that's right, then the process ought to have left some discoverable mark on the past. There ought to be some relationship, in history, between real individual creators and the other creative geniuses that came before, alongside, and after them. There also ought to be some patterns discoverable among the great currents of creativity that have swept through history.

One way of looking into this is to take actual creative individuals who have obtained historical distinction and then identify correlations using biographical and historical data. We already have all the data we need in the many published reference works; all we need to do is to operationalize the data by joining the dots. So we can start, for example, by identifying artists in a standard biographical dictionary. Next, we can assess the relative eminence of the artists using page counts, picture counts, and existing rankings. Then we can test for correlations between eminence and social relationships: here, influential or inspirational predecessors, contemporaries, and successors of various kinds. Finally, we can do the statistics to see what kind of connection there is between a great creator and his or her social world more broadly.[12]

Great artists, it turns out, tend to be deeply embedded in a mesh of social relationships. This in itself is not necessarily very surprising in the light of what we have seen, except insofar as it tends to defeat the stereotype of the poet in a garret, poor and alone. Where it gets interesting is in the type of relationships that come out as being important.

First of all, it is of no real significance for an artist to have another family member who is also a famous artist. If anything, the effect is negative. So, for example, having an eminent parent is negatively related to an artist's own personal eminence. Likewise, those with brothers or sisters who are eminent artists are *less* likely to be famous than those without. Artistic talent does not, it seems, run in families.

All other kinds of relationships have a positive impact: paragons (influencers), masters (teachers) in the preceding generation; rivals, collaborators, associates, friends, and co-pupils in the contemporaneous generation; apprentices and admirers in the succeeding generation.

What's most of value, though, is the finding that the relationships don't have to be personal or highly intimate to make a difference. Whereas in the Hans Krebs study, it was the teacher that made the difference, here a bigger impact can be seen coming from more remote predecessors who have influenced or inspired the artists from some historical distance.

How far is the pattern reflected in history? We find, for example, that the great Spanish artist Goya (1746-1828) – famous for works such as *The Third of May 1808*, depicting the massacre of Spaniards by

Napoleon's troops, and his darkly mythological *Saturn Devouring his Son* – had copied and been inspired by the works of both Velázquez (1599-1660) and Rembrandt (1606-1669) during his youth in Saragossa. As another example, we also find the great British artist J.M.W. Turner (1775-1851) – famous for that astonishing vortex of light and colour, *Snow Storm: Steam-Boat off a Harbour's Mouth*, and *Rain, Steam, and Speed* – had been inspired and influenced by the French painter Claude Lorraine (1600-1682).

Notice the length of time separating the painters from their progenitors – commonly around 150 to 200 years. The pattern repeats itself in literature. William Wordsworth (b. 1770) was inspired by Milton (b. 1608) – he even wrote a sonnet on it: 'London, 1802'. T. S. Eliot (b. 1888) took his inspiration, in turn, from the metaphysical poets of the early seventeenth century. Admittedly, given the scope of the subject matter, it would be no challenge to find exceptions. Artists of the Renaissance, for example, typically looked back well beyond a couple of centuries to the deep past of the Greek and Roman classical world. But there does seem to be a pattern.

So far, the statistics tell us several things. First, they tell us to look to the past for predecessors who can serve as models and sources of information.

Second, they tell us that the past to which we can look is not necessarily the immediate past but may well extend back two or more centuries. Inspiration, it seems, is not limited to lifetime transmission; it speaks across the gulfs of time.

We need mentors – it's hard to build from scratch in a total vacuum. But it may be that we also need distance from our inspirational figures, especially in creative fields, if we are not to be overborne by them and fall into the trap of mere imitation.

THE TRAGEDY OF ACHILLES

In the background of Shakespeare's *Troilus and Cressida* stride the great leaders and heroes of the Greek and Trojan forces, lined up to fight on the dusty plains of Troy. Yet the very greatest of these figures, Achilles, in a fit of pique at the disrespectful manner of Agamemnon, refuses to engage. The wisest of the Greeks, Ulysses, is sent to rectify the situation and bring Achilles back round to the Greek cause. No amount of argument or pleading will win him over; more sophisticated measures are called for, and Ulysses is the man for the job. First, he arranges matters so that the Greek leaders pass by Achilles, showing him little if any regard – Agamemnon, then Nestor, then Menelaus, and finally Ajax stroll past the great Achilles with barely a word of greeting. Achilles is confused and disconcerted – after all, isn't he the greatest of all the Greek warriors? Why, all of a sudden, should he be treated as a nonentity?

———

Next, Ulysses arranges for Achilles to see him reading a book. Still confused by what has happened, the great warrior Achilles strikes up a conversation with his fellow Greek, and the contents of the book become the talking point. Ulysses explains that the book is concerned with what it is that really makes a man:

> *A strange fellow here*
> *Writes me that man – how dearly ever parted,*
> *How much in having, or without or in –*
> *Cannot make boast to have that which he hath,*
> *Nor feels what he owes, but by reflection;*
> *As when his virtues shining upon others*
> *Heat them, and they retort that heat again*
> *To the first giver...*
>
> *I do not strain at the position –*
> *It is familiar – but at the author's drift,*
> *Who in his circumstances expressly proves*
> *That no man is the lord of any thing,*
> *Though in and of him there is much consisting,*
> *Till he communicate his parts to others;*
> *Nor doth he of himself know them for aught*

Till he behold them formed in th' applause
Where they're extended.
    Troilus and Cressida 3.3.95-102, 112-120

Don't be too distracted by the peculiarities of Elizabethan English – the gist of it all is in equal measure transparent and compelling. As Ulysses explains: whatever a man possesses – whether inwardly (in the form of personal talent or ability) or outwardly (in the form of appearance, wealth, or possessions) – counts for nothing unless it is recognized by others and that recognition is fed back to the person in question. A man cannot *know* what it is that he possesses unless this occurs; still more, he cannot properly be said to actually *have* anything at all without such recognition.

———

Shakespeare was striking at the heart of a truth that has become apparent through the course of this chapter. It's not only that human beings have a tendency to imitate other human beings, although that's part of it. Nor is it only that human beings can be primed or triggered in a predictable manner by stimuli coming from the outside, although that's part of it too. It's that without other people we are left destitute of a source from which to reference our meanings, standards, and values.

For Achilles, that meant no more hanging out in

his tent, sulking with his whore; for the rest of us, it means the possibility of a transformation admittedly less heroic, but not necessarily less profound.

BEING PRESENT

HOW LEONARDO DID *THE LAST SUPPER*

In the Church and Dominican convent of Santa Maria delle Grazie in Milan is the only remaining work by Leonardo Da Vinci that can still be visited *in situ*. Truth be told, the work – a fresco painted on the north wall of the refectory – has seen better days. Leonardo had not mastered the art of painting large murals and seems to have made a mistake in experimenting with a compromise between traditional tempera and oil. Even in Vasari's time, the painting had become essentially a 'dazzling stain'. In later centuries a door was cut into the wall, severing the feet of the pictured Christ. Napoleon's army stored horse fodder in the refectory, and the republican troops entertained themselves by throwing bricks at the apostles' heads. The refectory has survived at least two major floods and, at the end of World War II, the dropping of a bomb on its roof.[1]

I am talking, of course, about *The Last Supper*. The painting depicts the final meal that Jesus took with his disciples, when he revealed that one of the disciples would betray him. You probably need to actually go there to appreciate the way that Leonardo makes the fictional space of the painting expand the real space of the refectory, using the trick of perspective to increase the impression of depth. But the rest of it is there for all to see. There is the so-called secret geometry of the painting, which draws the viewer's eyes along the perspective lines to the vanishing point at the head of Christ. There is the compositional balance of the disciples, clustered into four groups of three, an arrangement which is varied only by Judas, darkly outlined, clutching a bag of silver to his breast, the one disciple to be shown shrinking away from the others. And there is the intrinsic drama of the scene: the expressions and gesture of shock, incredulity, remonstration, conjecture, denial, suspicion. Only Christ remains serene – resigned to the fact that he must die so that mankind can be saved.

What is interesting for us is not so much the brilliance of the work itself as the state of mind of the man who created it. Leonardo was, admittedly, an exceptional individual, but there was also something in his approach to work that is common to high achievers of all descriptions. As it happens, Leonardo was obliged to paint *The Last Supper* in the public space of the convent refectory, and as a result there are several eyewitness accounts of his manner of working. The best is that given by the nephew of the prior of the convent, Matteo Bandello. Bandello describes how Leonardo would arrive early in the morning, ascend the scaffold, and get straight to work. 'He sometimes stayed there from dawn to sundown,' wrote Bandello, 'never putting down his brush, forgetting to eat and drink, painting without pause. He would also sometimes remain two, three, or four days without touching his brush, although he spent several hours a day standing in front of the work, arms folded, examining and criticizing the figures to himself.'[2] Such accounts chime with those given by observers of that other great Renaissance painter, Michelangelo. Both men were, once engaged on a piece of work, entirely *absorbed* in the whole process.

Continuous activity, continuous attention, forgetting to eat and drink and sleep – these are signs of absorption that any onlooker can recognize. However, the kind of absorption that characterizes the pursuit of excellence is not always quite so obvious. Leonardo began *The Last Supper* in 1495 and by 1497 had completed the eleven apostles and the body of Judas. But why was there this delay with Judas' head? It had been a year since Leonardo had touched the painting, or even come to see it. Summoned to a meeting with his employer, the Duke of Ludovico, Leonardo nevertheless insisted that he had been working on it every day. How can that be, asked the Duke, if you do not go there? 'Your Excellency is aware that only the head of Judas remains to be done,' answered Leonardo, 'and he was, as everybody knows, an egregious villain. Therefore he should be given a physiognomy fitting his wickedness. To this end, for about a year if not more, night and morning, I have been going every day to the Borghetto, where Your Excellency knows that all the ruffians of the city live. But I have not yet been able to discover a villain's face corresponding to what I have in mind. Once I find that face, I will finish the painting in a day.' If we take Leonardo at his word –

and there is no evidence that he was telling anything but the truth – then he had *never* stopped working on the project in the entire time since starting it. Quite the reverse; his search for perfection had absorbed him, driving him every day and night to the roughest parts of the city in search of the raw material of his art.[3]

THE PSYCHOLOGY OF FLOW

A new understanding of the outstanding achievements of individuals like Leonardo was pioneered in Chicago in the 1960s, where a young psychology professor was embarking on what would become a lifetime's study of 'optimal experience'. Mihály Csíkszentmihályi had been fascinated by stories of artists who lost themselves in their work, and noticed that their most productive moments all had something in common: when engaged on a project that was progressing successfully, they would disregard hunger, fatigue, and discomfort until the project was finished – when they would rapidly lose interest and move on to the next challenge. In the course of the next forty years, Csíkszentmihályi observed and interviewed thousands of people to find out what it was that produced this state of 'full capacity'.[4]

Csíkszentmihályi believes that most of us spend most of our time in one of two extreme states – we

97

are either stressed by work or other obligations or bored as supine recipients of TV or other passive entertainments. What Csíkszentmihályi calls 'flow' constitutes another state altogether – flashes of 'intense living against this dull background'.[5] To investigate this, he devised the Experience Sampling Method (ESM). Respondents were provided with electronic devices and a questionnaire booklet, and researchers beeped them at random intervals seven times a day for a week. Each time they were beeped the respondents were required to fill out the survey books giving details of their activities and corresponding experiences and states of consciousness.

The results were decisive in their uniformity, varying little across cultures and settings. In a nutshell – and Csíkszentmihályi's conclusions are really quite simple – people found 'flow' when challenges were set that stretched (but did not overwhelm) existing skills, and when clear proximal goals were present. When challenges were too easy relative to existing skills, people experienced boredom; when challenges exceeded ability, the result was anxiety. And when low challenge met low skills, the predominant experience was apathy.

Csíkszentmihályi reckons that surgery is a typical 'flow' occupation. Surgeons have well-defined goals (to cut out a tumour, for example, or set a bone), and surgery provides immediate and continuous feedback. Most of all, surgery is challenging. The surgeon doesn't just have to make a success of the operation: he or she has to watch for the details, be neat and technically efficient, and coordinate a team of medical staff.

Csíkszentmihályi points to climbing as another flow activity. Here's how climber Doug Robinson, for example, describes the experience of climbing:

> Climbing requires intense concentration. I know of no other activity in which I can so easily lose all the hours of an afternoon without a trace. Or a regret. I have had storms creep up on me as if I have been asleep, yet I knew the whole time I was in the grip of an intense concentration, focused first on a few square feet of rock, and then on a few feet more, I have gone off across camp to boulder and returned to find the stew burned. Sometimes in the lowlands when it is hard to work I am jealous of how easily concentration comes in climbing. This concentration may be intense, but it is not the same as the intensity of the visionary periods; it is a prerequisite intensity.
>
> But the concentration is not continuous. It is often intermittent and sporadic, sometimes cyclic and rhythmic. After facing the successive few square feet of rock for a while, the end of the rope is reached and it is time to belay. The belay time is a break in the concentration, a gap, a small chance to relax. The climber changes from an aggressive and productive stance to a passive and receptive one, from doer to observer, and in fact from artist to visionary. The

99

climbing day goes on through the climb-belay-climb-belay cycle by a regular series of concentrations and relaxations. It is of one of these relaxations that Chouinard speaks. When limbs go to the rock and muscles contract, then the will contracts also. And at the belay stance, tied in to a scrub oak, the muscles relax and the will also, which has been concentrating on moves, expands and takes in the world again, and the world is new and bright. It is freshly created, for it really had ceased to exist. By contrast, the disadvantage of the usual low-level activity is that it cannot shut out the world, which then never ceases being familiar and is thus ignored. To climb with intense concentration is to shut out the world, which, when it reappears, will be as a fresh experience, strange and wonderful in its newness.[6]

There is, it has been said, a biological explanation for the intensified perception that comes to the climber. On the one hand, the exertion of the climb ramps up carbon-dioxide level (or 'oxygen debt') which manifests itself on the cellular level as lactic acid, a poison. On the other hand, there's adrenalin, an unstable compound that – if unused – soon begins to break down. Together they produce a chemical climate conducive to visionary experience.

Csíkszentmihályi, however, reckons it's more than that. Rock climbing, he says, has everything you would expect of a flow activity. Part of it is the concentration on a limited field; the climber cannot be anything but fully engaged if he wants to come back down in one piece. Then there's the responsiveness of the climb to the climber's ability level: the climber can adapt the climb to his skills, either pushing towards further challenges or easing off in the face of insurmountable difficulty. There's a feeling of competence and control – at least if the climber is doing it right. And – not least – there's a merging of action and awareness. Csíkszentmihályi likens the climb to a strip of film. When the action is too easy or too hard, the film stutters and the actor becomes aware of the borders of each frame. But when the difficulty is just right, action follows action in a fluid sequence and the individual frames merge into an unbroken flow.[7]

The experience of flow is addictive. Intense concentration on the present, merging of action and awareness, loss of self-consciousness, a sense of control, a feeling that time has passed quickly, and an experience of intrinsic 'worthwhileness' – these are all pleasing sensations that we will seek to repeat. This is at least one reason why flow leads to better performance. Once you have found flow in the carrying out of any activity – be it work, or art, or sport, or whatever – you will be inclined to seek a repetition of the experience. It will have given you intrinsic rewards that encourage persistence and return to an activity, which in turn will build greater and greater competence in that field. Sure enough, experimental studies have shown performance to be positively correlated to the experience of flow.

ACHIEVING FLOW

Climbing illustrates not only the subjective experience of flow; it also points to steps we can take to achieve it. For that we may turn to one of the most awe-inspiring of all activities that push human abilities to the edge – to what sportspeople know as 'free solo'.

The free soloist is a peculiar animal. Free soloists are climbing purists: they seek out the most demanding rock surfaces that they then proceed to climb with no rope, no harness, no bolts, and no safety gear. Free soloing is frankly a dangerous activity. It's probably the most extreme form of climbing imaginable. And in the world of free soloing, there is one name that commands instant respect: John Bachar.[8]

Bachar's climbing triumphs are the stuff of legend. The few climbs that have been filmed are astonishing. Take Bachar's free soloing of Leave it to Beaver, a giant chunk of granite in the Joshua Tree National Park. The climb is tough: it's rated 5.12a. (A 5.0-rated climb is the easiest; a 5.15-rated climb is the hardest. Fewer than 10 percent of climbers can ascend a 5.12 climb *with* a rope – and that figure declines to 5 percent for a 5.13 climb.) When you get in the range of a 5.12a, you are facing overhanging rocks, holds no bigger than a dime, and no places to rest. That's where Leave it to Beaver is on the scale.

Bachar looks every bit the Californian beach bum as he starts the climb: he's tanned and his blond hair is worn long. But that's where the likeness stops; no beach bum could even consider tackling the sheer face of granite that makes up this climb. Bachar's handhold for the first half of the climb is a narrow crack in the rock: it's along this crack that he crawls and from this crack that he swings – sometimes hanging from the rock with just one hand – to reach for the next hold. The second half of the climb is even more outrageous. The crack has gone and now it's just the Californian up against the rock, flat like a lizard, and with nothing much between him and certain death on the valley floor below. But Bachar *does* make it – and with real speed and grace. It's an astonishing performance.

Watch Bachar on the climb called Crack A Go Go and you're left with the same sense of awe. It's another vertical wall of granite in Yosemite threaded with narrow seams and pockets of rock upon which Bachar builds the climb. Bachar follows the seams with his fingertips, sometimes pulling on the rock horizontally for grip. It's not reckless; he's working the rock, feeling out each handhold as he goes. But he's also fast – and elegant. There's none of the hesitation you would expect given the self-evident danger of what Bachar is doing. 'I read somewhere if you fall over fifty feet and you land flat or something, your organs . . . that's when they start separating, tearing apart from each other inside your body. So after that I guess you have a pretty good chance of dying.'

Free soloing was not the future that anyone would have anticipated for the young Bachar. The climber's dad, a maths professor at UCLA, had always expected that his son – a grade A student – would at the least make it through college. The young Bachar wasn't taking: he had told himself that he was going to be the best climber in the world – and do whatever was necessary to get there. He dropped out of school in 1976 to 'put the same effort into climbing as I was going to put into being a professor'.

Bachar's dedication shone through what must have been difficult years. His father disavowed him for throwing it all away. (It would be many years later, when a student showed Bachar Sr. an article about the 'great climber John Bachar', that his father eventually came round.) Bachar's mother did what she could for her son, sending him the $50 a month child support paid by her father.

The training was intense. Bachar immersed himself in kinesiology and sports science. He ditched his unscientific pull-up/dip programme for a more scientific regimen of one-day-on, one-day-off training. This regimen was absolute; each day was set aside for a training or rest, and Bachar made no exceptions. At his best, he could do a two-arm pull-up with 140 pounds strapped to his belt and a one-arm pull-up with 12.5 pounds.

So there's the dedication. And there's the training. But what makes the free soloists really special is their breathtaking nerve in the face of real danger. When you free solo, you're not climbing a rock face that nobody else can climb; you're climbing in a way that nobody else would dare. The free soloist is distinguished from the lesser mortal by his *presence of mind*. 'I think maybe it's confidence,' said Bachar of those who couldn't do it. 'They are not confident in themselves that their body will do what their mind tells them to do every single time I think is a big part of it.' Or, as his friend and co-climber John Long put it: 'That perfect master thing that Bach was into which was I'm going to do this death-defying thing because I can.' It was, he concludes, 'a sort of quasi-mystical take on the whole thing. That was what he was into.'

―――――――

Here's the way Csíkszentmihályi presents the difference between the flow state and normal experience:

Normative Life	Rock-Climbing
Informational noise; distraction and confusion of attention	One-pointedness of mind
Nebulosity of limits, demands, motivations, decisions and feedbacks	Clarity and manageability of limits, demands, decisions, feedbacks
Severing of action and awareness	Merging of action and awareness
Hidden, unpredictable dangers; unmanageable fears	Obvious danger subject to evaluation and control
Carrot-and-stick preoccupation with exotelic, extrinsic material and social rewards; orientation towards ends	Process orientation; concern for autotelic, intrinsic rewards; conquest of the useless
Superficiality of concerns; thinness of meaning in the flatland	Dimension of depth up there; encounter with ultimate concerns[9]

It's a picture of two different worlds. There's the world of our normative existence: that's characterized by informational 'noise', a fogginess of expectations and unpredictability of danger, a 'carrot-and-stick' system of reward and punishment, and a pervading superficiality of concerns. The other world is one of clarity of limits, unambiguous danger, and intrinsic rewards.

——————

When climber John Long referred to Bachar's 'quasi-mystical' take on it, he may well have been thinking about one-pointedness in Buddhist thinking. One-pointedness is about keeping your mind concentrated on the task in hand. Anything ulterior to that task is to be ruthlessly pruned away from consciousness. Thoughts of personal benefit or loss, greedy thoughts, envious thoughts, lustful thoughts – these can all crowd around any action to distract and draw the mind away from its rightful object. Our minds are in this way corrupted by various forms of desire that take us away from the immediacy of what we are doing in the current moment. By fostering within ourselves a state of 'desirelessness' *vis-a-vis* what we are doing at the present, we are better able to bring about this one-pointedness of mind. The fundamental way in which this is to be done is by suspending thought about potential consequences and by detaching the object of attention from anything beyond itself. Psychological research tells a story that is largely at one with this philosophy: shift away from an internal focus (a focus on techniques, physiological state, or emotions) towards an *external* focus (a focus on the task itself) and our performance outcomes are dramatically improved.[10]

So how could Bachar do it without counterproductively striving for control of each movement? How could he look into the void, so to speak, without blinking?

To pull off free soloing Bachar-style was not just to make the climb; it was to make the climb *with panache*. 'Well, I don't know, climbing I think is about style as much as it getting to the summit. So anybody – a telephone repairman – can get to the summit [...] you know, but how you do it ... it's the whole game, you know. How you do it, what kind of style can you pull it off in.'

Bachar would start out modest:

When he solos, he tells himself that he's only going up 10 feet to check it out. He breaks a climb down into sections. 'If things ain't cool, no problem, I'll just go down.' If it does look good, he'll go another 10 feet, then reevaluate, always keeping the door open for backing off. 'It's the only way I don't get nervous.' This is the way he's done it for 30 years.

You can see the technique: breaking down the problem into potentially manageable chunks by bringing the attention to bear on the ten feet immediately ahead. Then, twenty feet or so off the ground, something would happen:

All of a sudden something clicks inside you. You're a different person. The amount of power that you have access to is much greater than you would have in everyday life. Your whole body kicks in – it's more the instinctual side of your being. You have these other powers that are available to you. I think we all have that capability inside of us, and when you free solo, you can tap into that. After a while, you start realizing you can turn your analytical mind off and connect with your animal mind, your instinctual mind. When you're free soloing a tough spot or a hard section, you let your analytical side disappear and you trust your animal instincts. You can do incredible things. All of a sudden, you focus like you've never focused before. That's a really addicting part of the whole thing because in a way, you get to see who you really are on a deep level, on an animal level, that you don't get to see in everyday life. It's really comforting to get in contact with your total being. It's so involving – you don't feel alone. You feel like you're plugged into some giant universal energy system or something. The rock doesn't feel like rock – it feels like your partner.

When you're doing it right, you're also completely focused:

You're so comfortable with this little circle of rock around you, with the consistency of the footholds and handholds, that's all that exists. The ground is not there. There's nothing else there except this fun little section of rock you have to move across and you're thinking about how to move across it smoothly, efficiently and gracefully. If you're doing it right, it should feel like you're bouldering five feet off the ground, you're so comfortable. But if there's a little thought in your head saying, 'I'm high off the ground,

109

what if I fall?' then you're not doing it right. Even if one per cent of your mind is thinking about falling or something else, then you don't belong there.[11]

It all comes down to a complete, intense focus on the immediate experience. Isn't this fundamentally the same thing that the Buddhists look for in their 'one-pointedness' of mind? And isn't it essentially the state achieved in the flow experience identified by Csíkszentmihályi?

ONE-POINTEDNESS AND PERFORMANCE UNDER PRESSURE

One-pointedness is a helpful concept because it highlights the importance of fixing attention on the task in itself and the removal of extraneous elements from consciousness. 'Flow' had focused on the *conditions* that give rise to peak performance – the point where capability and challenge are equally matched. One-pointedness can take us a step further by identifying a preferred *state of mind* focussed not on outcomes but fully engaged on the task at hand.

Cultivating this one-pointed state of mind does, however, ask more of us than we might at first suppose. One of the first steps is to make room for a new understanding of the relationship between motivation and result. This involves disillusioning ourselves of the stubborn preconception that increased motivation improves performance: the more effort we put in, we think, the better we will do. It is a belief that lies at the centre of so much of what we do as humans both in our personal lives (think schooling) and in society (think economic incentives). But is it helpful?

The question was addressed back in the early years of the twentieth century by Robert Yerkes and John Dodson. Yerkes and Dodson had observed rats that had been placed in a cage and forced repeatedly to choose between one of two passages. On each trial a white card was hung above one passage and a black card above the other. Rats choosing the white card would meet with a reward; those choosing the black card would meet with a shock at a certain intensity level. What was significant was that the rats learned to avoid the shocks when the shocks were at an intermediate – not a high – level of intensity. The Yerkes-Dodson law holds that motivation increases performance – but only up to this intermediate point. When arousal becomes too high, performance declines.[12]

By the middle of the century, it had become apparent that there was another process engaged when motivation increases. Increased emotional arousal, it was established, acts to reduce the range of 'cue utilization' – it narrows the focus of attention on a variety of dimensions. This can be detrimental for complex tasks or tasks involving insight or creativity. The use of monetary awards for problem-solving tasks, for instance, has been shown to have negative effects on performance.[13]

Performance failure under pressure is a phenomenon that has come to be known as 'choking'. Choking is seen especially in competitive sport, and there are two explanations for what is happening. It is possible that performance pressure increases self-consciousness and attention to step-by-step execution of skills, which disrupts automated processes. It is also possible that pressure causes thoughts about the situation and its importance to occupy working memory and distract attention from execution. Interestingly, while these two explanations have often been seen as incompatible, there is increasing awareness that they may both, in fact, describe a common phenomenon: in each case, pressure increases focus on task-irrelevant stimuli.[14]

———

There's no better way to end than to turn to the sportsmen and women themselves to hear how task-focus is maintained:

'You have to take away winning and the consequences of winning ... and [just] focus on the processes.'

'I used to expect much more of myself, but I have learned to accept that you do make mistakes.'

'I can't control what people say about me. So, I focus on the task, and what I work towards is for me ... no one else.'

'I identify things I can control ... I know what my processes are to reach my goal. I just concentrate on what I can control and forget about what I can't control. Simple.'

'I make an eagle ... do I suppress that or ride the wave? The best bit of advice I got about that was ... "what are you talking about!" It's too much thought. Neutral is the gear you should play the game in ... one shot after the next and that's it.'

'Positive doesn't work. Negative doesn't work. Neutral does. You focus on the skills, you complete the action.'

These are quotations from five elite golfers who excelled under pressure.[15] No doubt similar accounts could be heard from elite performers in all walks of life.

THE PATH TO EMEI

Emei Mountain is a spectacular place. The mountain was formed back in prehistory when the collision of the Indian and Eurasian sub-tectonic plates created a dramatic vertical uplift of land that had once been at the bottom of the sea. The rock that makes up the mountain comes from ten of the thirteen known geological periods, creating a multitude of colour effects: there is pinkish granite, purple and green shale, limestone, dolomite and basalt, and to top it off a layer of dark-red basaltic lava on the summit. Emei isn't the tallest mountain in the world by any means, but it is one of the most *vertical*: some of Emei's peaks and ridges drop a breathtaking 2,000 m to the valleys below.

It's not just the shape of Emei that makes it special – it's what you encounter once you get there. The dramatic verticality means that Emei is divided effectively into three climatic zones. At the base it's tropical, with an average temperature of 17.2° C, or 63° F. In the middle regions is the near-legendary 'sea of green'. Cedar, conifer, cypress, as well as more unusual flower-bearing trees – crab-apple, woody lotus, and cassia – are all there, as well as a total of 107 plants that are unique to Emei. At the top of the mountain it's cold, averaging only 3° C, or 37° F. Travellers 'look like frozen little ants', said the famous Song dynasty writer Su Shi. What he failed to mention is that most of the time you wouldn't even be able to see them – fog descends on the mountain for an average 323 days per year.

Emei has drawn pilgrims for many centuries. In China, mountains are often considered holy places, and Emei is one impressive mountain. Another reason, though, is mystery of Emei's 'precious light', an unusual optical effect that occurs on the summit under certain conditions. There has to be moisture in the air – raindrops, ice crystals, or snowflakes. The sun has to be shining from behind. And ahead of you there has to be a bank of fog or cloud onto which your shadow is projected. If all that occurs, you'll see a spectacular light effect – a globe of light with a centre of concentrated brightness and a multicoloured outer corona. The precious light isn't the only thing worth looking for on Emei, but it epitomizes just how exceptional the place is. One expert on Emei, James Hargett, puts it this way: 'I have come to realize that nothing about Emei shan is ordinary'.[16]

———

Up on Emei Mountain, on the path leading to Elephant Bathing Pool, is a temple that is known as 'Meeting Immortal Monastery'. There is an old folktale that has been told on those misty slopes about this monastery, a tale that is still told today.[17]

One day, long ago, a man was walking up the mountain between Elephant Bathing Pool and Nine Ancients Cavern. He was wearing nothing but a worn-out gown, his eyes were dim, and his face was pale with exhaustion. He staggered onwards as far as he was able but eventually could go no farther and fell to the ground through weariness. As it happened, an old woodcutter – bundles of firewood strapped to a pole across his shoulders – was at the same time making his way downhill, and he came across the old man lying collapsed on the ground.

'Good fellow, why are you lying here asleep on the mountain? If you wish to sleep, why do you not seek shelter and rest in one of the nearby monasteries?'

'I've come from afar in search of immortality,' replied the man. 'But I've searched the whole mountain and not managed to find a single immortal. I'm now penniless. I collapsed here through hunger and exhaustion.'

The old woodcutter roared with laughter. 'I've been cutting wood on this mountain longer than I can remember,' he said, 'and I have journeyed from the thickest forests to the highest peaks. In all these years I have never met an immortal. You had better forget this dream of yours and go home.'

'I have no money, I've not eaten in days, and there is no strength left in these old legs of mine,' replied the man. 'How on earth can I get home?'

'Don't worry. I'll take care of you,' said the old woodcutter. He set to work chopping off a branch of a nearby tree. When he had finished, he passed the branch to the man. 'Sit astride the branch,' he said, 'close your eyes, and you will be carried home.'

The man did as he was told. Lo and behold, within minutes he had been carried down to the base of the mountain just beneath Longevity Bridge. *Hold on,* thought the man. *Isn't this old woodcutter an immortal? How else could he have managed to get me back down the mountain?* Hunger and exhaustion all but forgotten, the man started back up the trail as fast as his aching body would carry him.

When he got there the old woodcutter had disappeared, and in his place was an old man with grey hair and silver beard. The old man had a basket over his shoulder and a small hoe in his hands, and was gathering medicinal herbs.

'Grandpa, did you see an old woodcutter just now?' he asked.

'Which one are you talking about?' asked the old herb-gatherer. 'There are several old woodcutters on the mountain.'

'The one who is an immortal!'

'Ho, ho!' laughed the old herbalist. 'All the old woodcutters on the mountain are immortals! They scale the mountain to earn a living cutting firewood, seeking neither power nor wealth. Don't you think they deserve to be called immortals?'

'Where do you live, Grandpa?' asked the man.

'I live in the depths of the white clouds.'

'The depths of the white clouds? Isn't that where the immortals live?'

'I dwell with many immortal sages and we are each of the same age.'

'So you are one of the immortals?'

'Though like an immortal I am not what I seem,

but more than the immortals is the joy that I glean,' said the old herb-gatherer.

The man was overjoyed to have finally found one of the immortals. He threw himself to the ground before the old man.

'I now know you to be a true immortal. I've travelled many a mile to find you. Please,' he begged, 'teach me how to obtain immortality.'

'I'll read a verse to you,' answered the old man. 'If you understand it, you will become an immortal.'

Then he spoke:

Seeking immortals the heights you did scale,
But such a quest is doomed to fail.
For while you sought the saints' domain,
Dearest to them is the world of men.

When he had finished chanting the verse, the old herbalist offered the man a herb from his basket to ease his hunger and sent him off back home. The herbalist then disappeared into the depths of the mountain forest.

As he made his way back down the mountain, the man pondered the words of the old herbalist. *Even the immortals love this mortal world!* he thought. *Then why should I strive so hard to become an immortal?* With that thought, he decided to begin the long journey home.

He would never again seek immortality.

What the old tale teaches us is something very profound: that enlightenment and transcendence are not necessarily to be found 'up there' or 'out there' but *in this very world in which we live*. The secret of immortality for the Buddhist and Daoist sages was to find the point at which the illusion of self was extinguished by a deep engagement with the here and now.

The man in the story searched high and low for the secret of immortality, but could never find it. Why? By thinking of immortality as something outside and beyond himself – some elixir, perhaps, or some magic spell – he was condemned to lose touch with the immediacy of his experience. Every footstep on the mountain, every heavenly sunrise or sunset, every glorious snowbound crag – all these experiences would be contaminated by extraneous thoughts ('How close am I to immortality?')

The woodcutter, on the other hand, sought for nothing unrelated to the task in hand. No thoughts of power, or wealth, or even immortality for him – just the sensation of axe in hand, just the sound of sharpened metal cutting through wood, just the weight of the pole across his shoulders as he bore the wood down the mountain. In those moments of complete focus he found the immortality that comes when 'self' merges with task and object.

That's why immortals look like this:

It's a painting (now housed in the National Palace Museum in Taipei) by Liang Kai ('The Madman') of an immortal.[18] Sketched out using lighter and then darker washes of ink, the figure seems to be emerging from an aery nothingness into this world, before heading back into the nothingness from whence he came. The boundaries between himself and the world around him have dissolved entirely.

True, this is not immortality in the traditional sense of infinite life span. What it is, though, is a continuity of experience that transcends ego. It's what the Buddhists call 'one-pointedness' and what Csíkszentmihályi called flow. It's the focus of mind on the task at hand.

And it's what makes us great.

THINKING
DIFFERENTLY

HARVARD BULL

How do our most generative individuals think? Is there a style or manner of thinking that increases our overall effectiveness? How far does intellect matter anyway?

Let's begin to answer that by taking a journey back to Harvard University in the 1940s. The story begins one rainy November day in the lobby of Memorial Hall, where a certain mathematics junior ('Mr. Metzger') stood waiting to take part in a drama rehearsal.[1] For some reason, Metzger was the only student there that day; nobody else seemed to have turned up for the rehearsal. Pondering for a few moments whether the rehearsal could have been cancelled without his knowledge, Metzger was intrigued by students filing into the Great Hall opposite and taking seats at the tables within. They were about to sit for one of the University's many assessments.

Among the students crossing the lobby to enter the Great Hall was a familiar face – one of Metzger's friends. Metzger approached him and asked him what exam it was they were about to take. 'Oh, Soc. Sci. something-or-other,' replied the friend as he ambled towards the Hall. 'It's about Modern Perspectives on Man and Society and All That.' Metzger expressed an interest and wanted to know what books they had read. They chatted for a while about the course. Before they knew it, they were both in the Great Hall. 'Take your seats, please,' came a stern voice from beside them. Metzger's friend, naturally, obeyed; on an impulse Metzger (who should not, of course, have been there in the first place) sat down too. The proctor put blue answer books before them. Another proctor then presented them with copies of the test.

Metzger found himself seated in a social science examination, the substance of which he knew nothing. Now, most of us in this situation would shyly raise up a hand, notify the proctor that a mistake had been made, and ask to be excused. But Metzger didn't do that. Instead, overwhelmed with curiosity and glee, he invented the name 'George Smith' for himself, scribbled it on the blue book, and addressed the first question.

As a mathematics major with no knowledge of

the social sciences, Metzger admittedly struggled a bit with the 'objective' or 'spot' questions of the test: he would later find himself awarded with only a D for this component. The essay question was a different matter. Candidates were offered a choice of two books: Margaret Mead's *And Keep Your Powder Dry* or Geoffrey Gorer's *The American People*. Two critical comments (one positive and one negative) were offered on each book, and students were required – as they so often are – to 'discuss'. Metzger had read neither of the books, but plumped for the latter option 'because the title gave me some notion as to what the book might be about'. He set to work.

Metzger started with the author's name 'Geoffrey', and proceeded on the basis that Gorer was born into an 'Anglo-Saxon' culture, probably English, but without doubt English-speaking. Having heard that the second author, Margaret Mead, was a social anthropologist, Metzger then inferred that Gorer was most likely the same. These simple assumptions allowed him to formulate the central question that he would address in his essay: 'What are the problems inherent in an anthropologist's observation of a culture that is his own, or nearly his own?' Metzger spun out his analysis of this problem with reference to cultural relativity and the relation of observer to observed, assessing as he did so the kind of objectivity that might accrue as a result of an anthropologist's training. It was an outrageous attempt to spin an essay out of virtually nothing.

It is Metzger's conclusion that really displays his talent. Gorer's *The American People* did indeed, according to our mathematician-cum-anthropologist Metzger, offer a range of 'objective' and even 'fresh' insights into the nature of American culture. 'At the same time,' he somberly warned, 'these observations must be understood within the context of their generation by a person only partly freed from his embeddedness in the culture he is observing, and limited in his capacity to transcend those particular tendencies and biases which he himself has developed as a personality in his interaction with his culture since his birth.' You can tell that Metzger is really going for it now. His pen is flowing; his mind is racing ahead of itself; he feels the inspiration. 'In this sense the book portrays as much the character of Geoffrey Gorer as it analyzes that of the American people.' We almost want Metzger to give us an *encore*. And he does not disappoint, adding these final few words: 'We are thus much the richer.' You can almost picture the look of glee on his face as he scribbled his conclusion and handed his paper to the unknowing proctors.

We are thus much the richer.

Who knows what Metzger hoped to achieve that day in Harvard's Great Hall? He had quite unnecessarily decided to compete against students in a field of which he knew nothing. He didn't stand a chance.

Or did he?

Metzger's friend went to pick up his blue book a few days later. Like many of his classmates, the friend had scored an unimpressive C . When he picked up the blue book completed by a certain 'George Smith' (that's Metzger), however, he noticed that the grade awarded for the essay was a much more impressive A–. In the margin of Metzger's book was a note written by the assessor. 'Excellent work,' it read. 'Could you have pinned down these observations a bit more closely? Compare in . . . .' Metzger had aced the assessment.

Of course, it was never going to be as straightforward as all that. News got out, as it inevitably would, and Metzger was brought to the attention of the University authorities. He had broken the rule, among others, that no student may attend an examination in a course in which he is not enrolled. Metzger stood in danger of probation. Disciplinary proceedings were commenced, and the Administrative Board of Harvard College was required to rule on the issue.

How was the Board to deal with the Metzger problem? At best, we would think, they would have looked on the episode as childish pranksterism and admonish Metzger accordingly. At worst they may have taken serious affront: here was a student who had challenged the system and thrown up serious questions about the accuracy and integrity of their assessments. However it was looked upon, things were not likely to come out well for Metzger.

In fact, nothing of the sort occurred. The members of the Board were not only not affronted by Metzger's exploit, they were 'delighted' by it. So when one of the more legalistic members of the Board noticed that the rule applied only to 'examinations' – and that Metzger had not intruded on an examination at all, merely a one-hour 'test' – the prankster was home and dry. Metzger was off the hook.

Why had the University come to Metzger's aid? This was addressed years later by another Harvard staff member, William Perry. The Harvard people had, Perry revealed, correctly identified Metzger's essay as 'bull'. But 'bull', as it turns out, was something of which they approved. It showed the ability to reflect and expand upon the (admittedly limited) information at hand. What the Harvard professors were more concerned about was not 'bull' but rather its uncreative opposite – what Perry calls *cow*. 'Cow' is 'data, however relevant, without relevancies'. It is hypothesis understood as certain fact; answers sought where questions should first be asked; multiple perspectives rejected in favour of dogma.

Cow may be careful and diligent, so it probably seems a little unfair to prefer bull. But there is one key difference that gives bull the legitimate edge: bull acknowledges its own fallibility. In cow thinking, for example, a statistic becomes a fact. Bull, on the other hand, shows a healthy skepticism towards 'facts' in general. For the producer of cow, knowledge is a prison, and additional knowledge can only make the bars of that prison stronger. For proponents of bull, all knowledge takes form as hypothesis – and refutable hypothesis at that.

Einstein once said that imagination is more important than knowledge. Harvard, in its dealing with Mr. Metzger, showed that it agreed.

In this chapter, we find out why Harvard may have been right.

WHY CONTRARIANS DO BETTER

Original thinking is something we may approve of in principle and yet recoil from in practice. It's potentially disruptive. It challenges the status quo. It's incompatible with the 'just get it done' attitude that we take with us to the workplace and beyond. Can we start, then, by pointing to occasions when it has demonstrably led to better practical outcomes?

—————

Let's cast our minds back to the financial crisis of 2007-2008. This was an event that took by surprise so many people that it has famously been called a 'black swan' event. And yet not all were caught off guard. During the same short period, a man called John Paulson pulled off the greatest and perhaps most controversial trade in financial history. That year Paulson's firm, Paulson & Co., made a heart-stopping $15 billion. Of that $15 billion, Paulson personally was able to take a cut of nearly $4 billion. That has been calculated, according to one observer, to exceed the gross domestic products of several nations. It amounts to an income of more than $10 million a day.[2]

There wasn't anything in Paulson's background that spoke of success of anything other than the conventional kind. After graduation, Paulson went from Boston Consulting Group to Odyssey Partners to Bear Stearns to Gruss & Co. before starting his own firm, Paulson & Co., to focus on merger arbitrage. Using the skills he had honed in his years at Bear, he figured he could bet upon companies that he thought were likely to be acquired or benefit from competing take-over offers; he also learned to bet *against* companies set to be taken over when it appeared to him the take-over would fall through. It was what Paulson knew and what he was good at – his fund delivered respectable returns – but it would not be enough to get him into the big time. That would take something more.

When the time came, however, Paulson was ready.

Wall Street's great gift to Paulson was mortgage securitization. Financial firms, riding the wave of year-on-year increases in house prices, bought up home mortgages and other kinds of debt. They then repackaged the debt and sold it on to investors hungry for more and more exposure. Investors who were hungry but not *that* hungry could buy into the higher-rated slices or 'tranches' of the debt; those who were *really* hungry could buy into the lower-rated tranches offering higher returns.

Paulson did something that seems – in retrospect – very simple. He bought insurance (credit default swaps) on these investments – so, when the housing market collapsed, his insurance would rise in value. Paulson then followed through on his logic, looking for other institutions tarnished by the rash spate of mortgage lending. And when he worked out that the banks and financial firms had held on to a substantial portion of this toxic debt, he bought insurance covering their failure too.

He bought just about as much as he and his firm could afford.

When the housing market tanked, Paulson became an exceptionally rich man.

—————

In retrospect, Paulson's trade seems obvious. Who would not want to buy insurance on toxic debt and the zombie banks that held it?

What they did at Paulson & Co. in fact shows just how obvious it really should have been. Paulson and his team began by working out a trend line for the housing data they had gathered. Next, they ordered data on real estate going back all the way to 1975. They discounted for inflation. Finally, they performed a regression analysis to get their trend line for the whole period.

And here's what they discovered. From 1975 to 2000, house prices had climbed a mere 1.4 percent per year after taking into account inflation. From 2000 to 2005, however, prices had soared at a rate of over 7 percent per year. House prices were 40 percent over where they should have been according to historic trends. What was more, each time housing had taken a hit in the past, it had fallen down through the trend line. The inevitable conclusion: there would be a brutal correction on its way.

So it *should* have been obvious. But it wasn't.

The traders from Goldman Sachs weren't convinced by Paulson's analysis. Josh Birnbaum, Goldman's top trader of CDS protection, asked to come to Paulson's office. 'If you want to keep selling, I'll keep buying,' he said. 'Look, we've done the work and we don't see them taking losses.' The experts at Bear Stearns were also unimpressed. 'You guys are good customers and we're concerned about you. You guys need to do more research on historical price appreciation,' they told Paulson. When Paulson wanted to know how they had come to their conclusions, he was stonewalled by the Bear Stearns team. 'Our models are fine,' said one. 'We've been doing this for twenty years.'

The illusion of endlessly increasing house prices

went right to the heart of the system. This less-than-prescient analysis was typical: 'Fundamental factors – including solid growth in incomes and relatively low mortgage rates – should ultimately support demand for housing. We will follow developments in the subprime market closely. However, at this point, the troubles in the subprime sector seem unlikely to spill over to the broader economy or the financial system.' That was as late in the day as June 2007. And the speaker of those words was none other than the chairman of the Federal Reserve, Mr. Ben Bernanke.

MARGINALITY AND EMINENCE

What Paulson was doing was betting against the majority. That's something that's not only not unusual among highly successful people – it's actually highly characteristic of them.

If you want to know how great people think, it would be hard to do much better than to go back to Dean Keith Simonton. Simonton is Professor Emeritus of the Department of Psychology at the University of California (Davis) and he specializes in the study of genius, creativity, and leadership. One of Simonton's many achievements has been to pioneer the quantitative study of genius using archival data. Rather than merely theorize about genius, Simonton dug deep into historical sources to search for what it was that made some thinkers great while others fell into obscurity.

Simonton began by compiling a list of 2,012 Western thinkers representing over two dozen nationalities and spanning a time period from 580 BC to 1900 AD.[3] For each of these thinkers, he then established a measure of 'achieved eminence'. Simonton did this by combining existing ratings with entries in encyclopedias and histories: a thinker could be awarded one point per page in Marias' *History of Philosophy*, for example, or two points for a separate entry in the *Encyclopedia of Philosophy*. The higher a thinker had been ranked by scholars and the more extensive the commentary on that thinker, the higher his relative score.

Once that had been done, it was a matter of establishing the individual characteristics that were correlated with achieved eminence.

What Simonton expected was roughly as follows. First, he anticipated that eminence would be a positive function of philosophical *breadth*: thinkers who dealt with the full spectrum of philosophical questions were expected to do better than one-issue advocates. Second, he expected that eminence would be a negative function of *extremism*: we generally prefer individuals having attitudes and beliefs similar to our own – and that's not likely to happen for those promoting extreme or minority opinions. Third, Simonton expected – given the existing evidence showing that we seek 'balance' or 'consonance' in our own belief systems – that eminence would be positively related to a given thinker's philosophical *consistency*.

Simonton also expected to see a correlation between achieved eminence and the extent to which a thinker embodies the spirit of his age. He put forward two further hypotheses. First, he proposed that eminence would be a positive function of *representativeness*: what sets the most eminent thinkers apart, reasoned Simonton, was not necessarily the novelty of their ideas but the extent to which they were able to express the mores and intellectual fashions of the time. Second, he proposed that eminence would also be a function of *precursiveness*. Were the truly eminent thinkers successful because they were precursors of a future *zeitgeist*?

The results? Simonton got it right on the first count – eminence *was* related to philosophical breadth. But on every other count he was spectacularly *wrong* – albeit wrong in a very helpful way. To summarize Simonton's hypotheses (alongside the results of his study):

- *Eminence is a negative function of extremism.* **Wrong.** Extremism had a *positive* association with achieved eminence; we rate thinkers more highly when they express *minority* (not majority) viewpoints.
- *Eminence is a positive function of consistency.* **Wrong.** Consistency was more characteristic

of minor thinkers than their more famous colleagues. Major thinkers do not associate different positions across different issues.

- *Eminence is a positive function of representativeness.* **Wrong.** Only lesser intellectuals adhere to the *zeitgeist.* The great thinker is not a spokesman for his age.
- *Eminence is a positive function of precursiveness.* **Wrong.** Precursiveness has a statistically significant *negative* association with achieved eminence. Eminent thinkers are more likely to adhere to the beliefs of the *previous* generation than they are to promote those of the future *zeitgeist.*

Was the study a failure? Absolutely not. What Simonton dug up was something far more interesting than he could have expected.

The truly eminent thinkers of Simonton's study were advocates of minority positions that were not generally accepted by the societies they lived in or even the societies to come. They were marginals. They were retrogrades. They weren't even particularly consistent.

They saw things differently.

COGNITIVE COMPLEXITY AND THE SUCCESSFUL REVOLUTIONARY

Now consider the following individuals:

Thomas Jefferson
John Adams
Oliver Cromwell
John Lilburne
V. I. Lenin
L. D. Trotsky
Mao Tse Tung
Lin Piao
Fidel Castro
Ernesto 'Che' Guevara

While it's likely that you're more familiar with some of the names than with others, you'll recognize that they were all revolutionaries. Jefferson and Adams were both American presidents who had been involved in the composition of the Declaration of Independence. Cromwell was the leading figure in the English Civil War; he went on to become the Lord Protector of the short-lived English Commonwealth. Lenin and Trotsky, Mao, and Castro were leaders of the revolutions in Russia, China, and Cuba, respectively. At the 'less familiar' end of the spectrum are John Lilburne (English firebrand and radical), Lin Piao (Chinese revolutionary and designated successor of Mao Tse Tung), and Che Guevara (Cuban guerilla and author of the *Motorcycle Diaries*).

Now consider which of them were successful and which were failures. Usually this kind of assessment is difficult. It's the old chestnut of how to define success: is it defined by wealth, power, achievement, or happiness? And how do we measure these things anyway? Fortunately, revolutionaries make this easy for us; their trajectories have an 'all or nothing' quality. Some of them achieve high office and stay there until they voluntarily step down or die a natural death (these are the successes); others are forcibly removed or otherwise come to a sticky end (these are the failures). Each of our revolutionaries above can be categorized along these lines:

Revolutionary	Outcome
Thomas Jefferson	Success
John Adams	Failure
Oliver Cromwell	Success
John Lilburne	Failure
V. I. Lenin	Success
L. D. Trotsky	Failure
Mao Tse Tung	Success
Lin Piao	Failure
Fidel Castro	Success
Ernesto 'Che' Guevara	Failure

Obviously this leads to some seemingly anomalous

outcomes (with the unpleasant Lenin rated as more successful than our romantic motorcyclist-revolutionary Che Guevara), but the method has the rare virtue of having identified an objective measure of success. Lenin *did* make it all the way to a natural death while he was still in power; Che Guevara *was* killed leading a band of unsuccessful revolutionaries in Bolivia.

What makes some revolutionary leaders successful and others not? The answer may lie in the little known concept of 'cognitive complexity'. Cognitive complexity isn't exactly contrarianism, and it isn't exactly bull thinking, but it bears some startling similarities to both. Some individuals, goes the theory, are more cognitively complex than others: they tend to respond in an open and flexible way to stimuli; they search for novelty and further information; and they are able to consider multiple points of view simultaneously. (Their more 'cognitively simple' cousins are situated at the other end of the spectrum: they tend to evaluate stimuli in a more rigid manner; reject information that is not obviously compatible with their point of view; and are submissive in the face of authority.)

One of the tests that researchers have used to measure cognitive complexity gives a good idea of what lies at the heart of the idea. What you do is to analyze a person's thinking (as expressed in an essay, say, or a letter) by looking at the extent to which they are able to break away from rigid 'either/or' categories. You can score a text on this basis as follows: does it show *polarized contrast* (that's where two points of view are treated as polar opposites), *qualified contrast* (where two points of view are compared with the implication that they are not simple opposites), or *integrative comparison* (where a commonality between two divergent points of view is identified)?[4]

So how do our revolutionaries fare? When researchers analyzed their writings, they found something very curious. The successful leaders showed marked and significant increases in cognitive complexity after they had come to power; however, this shift was barely noticeable for the unsuccessful leaders who stayed at a relatively low level of complexity despite the change in circumstances. Jefferson, Cromwell, Lenin, Mao, and Castro were all able to adapt their thinking post-revolution to the new complexities they must have faced as leaders (rather than as ideologues and rabble-rousers). The unsuccessful revolutionaries, on the other hand, were unable to step up to the mark. Their thinking remained simple throughout.[5]

It's an old piece of research, but it still tells us something very interesting. For prospective revolutionaries out there, it's fine to be conceptually simple: there's a lot to be said for straightforward dogged single-mindedness when it comes to overthrowing an existing regime. For prospective *leaders*, on the other hand, a whole different skillset is required: factions must be reconciled, diverse considerations taken into account, and changing circumstances responded to in a flexible way. The world no longer appears in black and white but in many different shades of grey. Those who are unable to adapt their thinking are not likely to fare well or last long.

A HIGHER LEVEL CONTRARIANISM

Let's reconsider Paulson's success in the light of the cognitive complexity approach.

Was there anything very complex about Paulson's trade and the thought that went into it? Why was it any more complex than that of the Goldman and Bear Stearns traders who wanted to take bets in the other direction? Wasn't it simply a matter of better research and better judgment?

Look at the specifics of what Paulson actually had to do to pull off his trade.

First, he had to work out not just the fundamentals of the housing and mortgage markets to identify mispricing of the securities. He also had to identify the sentiments of those who thought differently from himself. Buying CDS contracts is buying insurance; it's what those in the business call a negative-carry trade because it means making regular payments with no returns until the default actually occurs. If investor sentiment – or government intervention – continues to push the market upwards in the face of negative fundamentals, the CDS purchaser can be bled dry before payback. It's not good enough, therefore, just to be right; you've got to be able to predict when the market will turn. And, to do that, you've got to be able to enter the mindset of those who are *wrong*.

Paulson also had to anticipate the effect of his own behaviour on the market. If other investors caught on, they might start to purchase the same insurance themselves and drive up the cost. 'It doesn't take much for hedge-fund managers to catch on, and it was such a glaring mispricing, I was afraid too much attention would cause it to disappear,' says Paulson. 'I didn't tell some potential investors the whole story, with all the details, because the more I discussed it, the more likely it would go away.' Paulson accordingly had to anticipate how those who were wrong might begin to recognize they were wrong and come belatedly to the right conclusion – and in so doing ruin his trade.

And Paulson ran the risk of being *so right that he was wrong*. When he identified the fragility of not just the securities but also the banks that held them, he quite rightly made bets against those banks as well. But what would happen if he was right and the banks *did* fail? What would happen to the value of all his insurance when it was the banks that would have to pay up on it in any event? Paulson and his team had to shift the winnings from the ailing investment banks into more secure investments – institutional Treasury-bond funds – at exactly the right moment. In other words, Paulson had to gauge the collateral consequences of his being right.

At each step of the way it had been a matter not of taking one position against another but of looking at the problem in the round: a kind of higher-level contrarianism.

Complexity in Action

Let's return to the idea of cognitive complexity but take it one step further. Let's go beyond the level of the individual to society as a whole. To do that, let's consider what cognitive complexity has to tell us about nations in conflict.

Peter Suedfeld, one of the main proponents of the 'complexity' theory, has looked specifically at the complexity levels displayed by the main protagonists in two international conflict situations that ended very differently: first, the 1914 crisis, which led to the bloodbath of the First World War; and second, the 1962 Cuban Missile Crisis in which a dispute between the United States and the USSR over the placement of missiles in Cuba – a dispute that could so easily have led to all-out war – was successfully resolved through diplomatic means.[6]

It was another case of raiding the archives. Suedfeld dug out records of speeches and diplomatic communications made by leading decision-makers in the two crises. For the 1914 crisis, he selected the following: for Great Britain, Sir Edward Grey (Foreign Secretary) and Sir Arthur Nicolson (Permanent Under-Secretary for Foreign Affairs); for France, Rene Viviani (Premier and Minister for Foreign Affairs) and J.-B. Bienvenu-Martin (Acting Minister for Foreign Affairs); for Germany, Kaiser Wilhelm and his Chancellor; for Austria-Hungary, Emperor Franz Joseph and Count Leopold Berchtold (Minister for Foreign Affairs); and, for Russia, Czar Nicholas and S. D. Sazonov (Minister for Foreign Affairs). For the 1962 crisis, only two countries, the United States and the USSR, were involved, so things were a little easier. For the United States, Suedfeld picked John F. Kennedy and Dean Rusk (Secretary of State). For the USSR, it would be Nikita Krushchev, Andrei Gromyko (Minister for Foreign Affairs), and the then Ambassador to the United Nations, Vladimir Zorin.

Suedfeld wanted to gauge the complexity of the main protagonists not only at the 1914 and the 1962 crisis points, but also at two time phases (preliminary and climax) for each crisis. This would not only reveal the relative level of complexity of the key players, but also tell us something about the trajectory of that complexity level. How complex was their thinking at the critical moment? And was it getting more complex – or less?

One feature of the results was clear: the average

complexity score for the nations involved in the 1914 crisis was substantially lower than the average score for those nations involved in the 1962 crisis. The average complexity score for the Europeans just prior to the First World War was 1.99; the average complexity scores for the two superpowers prior to the Cuban Missile Crisis was 5.42. But it's not just that. There was also a noticeable (and statistically significant) *dip* in the scores between the preliminary phase and the climax phase for the 1914 crisis, and an even more noticeable (and likewise statistically significant) *uplift* in the complexity scores of the superpowers in the lead-up to the Cuban Missile Crisis.

To what extent are these results generalizable? World War I and the Cuban Missile Crisis – tragic as the former was and the latter may have been – were triggered by diplomatic and strategic considerations. Does cognitive complexity also have a role to play in the most deep-rooted and enduring of hostilities?

The Arab-Israeli conflict has without doubt been one of the bloodiest and most protracted of the last century. From the declaration in 1947 by the United Nations of a partitioned state in Palestine, it's been a history of war: sporadic, intermittent war but no less bitter for that. There's war in 1948: that's when the armies of Egypt, Lebanon, Syria, Jordan, and Iraq invaded the partitioned territory and when the Israeli Defense Force pushed back to effect an extension of Israeli borders. There's war in 1956: that's when, in response to the Egyptian nationalization of the Suez Canal, Israel invaded the Sinai Peninsula with British and French support before being pressured by the United States and the United Nations into a ceasefire. There's war in 1967: that was the Six-Day War, when Israel's air force swept through Egypt, Jordan, and Iraq, all but destroying the forces that were mobilized (once again) against them. Then there's war in 1973: that's when Syria and Egypt launched a surprise attack on Israel during Yom Kippur.

Researchers have charted the mean levels of conceptual complexity over the period as coded by scholars based upon speeches made by the Israelis ('Israel') and the Egyptians/Syrians ('UAR') in the UN General Assembly and Security Council.[7] When you follow the trajectories you see a story of human tragedy and suffering that runs in parallel to the cognitive complexity of the key players. Cognitive complexity drops sharply in the year 1947-48 (that's the year of the joint invasion of Israel by the Arab nations), it again drops sharply for the Israelis in 1955-56 (that's the year of the Suez crisis), it drops *very* sharply in 1966-67 (that's the Six-Day War), and it drops slowly at first but then more steeply in the years leading up to 1973 (that's the year of the Yom Kippur attack).

Here's what stands out: in the year preceding each conflict, the cognitive complexity of the participants – as reflected in the speeches at the UN – falls significantly. Or, to put it more broadly, outbreaks of violence are preceded by unusually low levels of complexity in international debates. It's not just that the antagonists have become more hostile or more aggressive, strictly speaking. It's simply that they have become less complex – less able to distinguish shades of grey, less able to see the various dimensions of a problem, less able put the fragments of a problem together to reach an integrated solution.

THE SWANSONG OF A ONETIME TRADER

Paulson's great trade brought great benefits – to him. For the rest of us it's another matter entirely. Some lost their jobs. Some lost their homes. Everybody paid – and will pay – more tax. It sticks in the gullet. Our contrarian is, after all, no role model. Some consider the Paulson and other 'short-sellers' to be little more than financial birds of prey swooping in to feed off the difficulties of the weak and the vulnerable.

But is that quite right?

Financial trades are voluntary agreements. Those who took the opposite side of Paulson's trades were happy to accept his ongoing payments while the housing market held up; when the market collapsed, it was time for Paulson to cash in. You can't blame the insured because they make a claim on the insurer.

Paulson has often been puzzled by the faith that we have put in mortgages and the new-fangled securities that sprang out of them. 'It was obvious that a lot of the stuff ... was practically worthless at the time of issuance,' he says. Paulson still finds it 'perplexing' that the banks could not see this danger and that so many were prepared to place unconditional trust in Wall Street.[8]

So what would have happened if there had been more people with Paulson's cast of mind in positions where they could have made a difference? What if the complexity of his thought – so to speak – had been prevalent throughout the political and financial community in the years leading to the financial crisis? Would that really have led to widespread predatory lending? Or would it have meant that lending was done with more respect for the real value of the property securing the loans?

One of the other large-scale buyers of CDS protection was a young American called Andrew Lahde. Lahde, who profited from his trades to the tune of $100 million for his clients and $10 million for himself, voiced his exasperation in an open letter penned in late October 2008.[9] It was his swansong to the world of financial trading that had made him a rich man:

October 27, 2008

Today I write not to gloat. Given the pain that nearly everyone is experiencing, that would be entirely inappropriate. Nor am I writing to make further predictions, as most of my forecasts in previous letters have unfolded or are unfolding. Instead I am writing to say goodbye. [...]

I was in this game for the money. The low-hanging fruit, i.e., idiots whose parents paid for prep school, Yale, and then Harvard MBA, was there for the taking. These people who were (often) truly not worthy of the education they received (or supposedly received) rose to the top of companies such as AIG, Bear Stearns, and Lehman Brothers and all levels of our government. All of this behavior supporting the Aristocracy only ended up making it easier for me to find people stupid enough to take the other side of my trades. God bless America. [...]

I will let others try to amass nine, ten, or eleven-figure net worths. Meanwhile, their lives suck.

Bitter it does sound. But is there not some sense in blaming – if blame there must be – not the likes of Paulson and Lahde but those who took the other sides of their trades?

DON'T BE BORING: CROP ROTATION

All men are boring.

149

Boredom is the root of all evil.

The gods were bored so they created man; Adam was bored because he was alone, so Eve was created; Adam and Eve then found that they were bored as a couple, so Cain and Abel were given life, but with the inevitable result that the entire family was now bored; at last, whole populations came into being – to find nothing but boredom awaiting them. It was out of that boredom that was hatched the idea of building a tower so high it reached the sky – the legendary Tower of Babel – but that idea is itself the height of boredom. The Romans had it right; to stay the inevitable decline of their civilization, they had the good sense to give the people what they wanted, which was nothing more than what they needed to keep them fed and to keep away the boredom – bread and circuses.

At least that's what nineteenth-century Danish philosopher Søren Kierkegaard had to say about it.[10] In his monumental work *Either/Or*, Kierkegaard marvels at the inconsistency of man, who when choosing a nursemaid for his children would quite obviously take into consideration her ability to keep the children entertained, yet are willing to tolerate the most insufferable bores in both private and public life. 'Were one to demand divorce on the on the grounds that one's wife was boring, or a king's abdication because he was boring to look at, or a priest thrown out of the land because he was boring to listen to, or a cabinet minister dismissed, or a life-sentence for a journalist because they were dreadfully boring, it would be impossible to get one's way.' The prevalence of boredom can only create opportunities for all kinds of mischief. 'What wonder,' thinks Kierkegaard, 'that the world is regressing.'

Kierkegaard came up with his own solution to this boredom and called it 'crop rotation'. The metaphor is an agricultural one: just as farmers rotate crops by changing the method of cultivation and type of grain on a given patch of land, so we as humans should change our way of looking at things so as 'to look at things you saw before, from another point of view'. This is to be contrasted to the 'vulgar' method of change, which consists merely of endless variation: endless travel from place to place, endless consumption of different cuisines, endless replacement of one thing with another. No – what is required is to cultivate *intensive* rather than *extensive* change, to change one's method of perception, understanding, and behaviour, not merely to change the external things with which one comes into contact. In fact, external limitations can be helpful in this process as they make inventiveness a necessity: 'The more you limit yourself, the more resourceful you become. A prisoner in solitary confinement for life is most resourceful, a spider can cause him much amusement.'

We are to enjoy all pleasures in moderation and never bind ourselves too strongly to the past. We are also to avoid the bonds of friendship, of marriage, and of professional or vocational responsibility, because they all limit an individual's freedom. The prohibition is not absolute: what is to be avoided is not friendship or love *per se*, but friendship and love in as much as they are binding obligations that prevent free action or impose customary rules on behaviour. Professional responsibility too is dangerous because the positions and titles that promotion brings tie you into a role over which you have little control.

Avoiding boredom, ultimately, comes down to appreciating the *arbitrariness* of things; the eye with which we look at reality must constantly change. We might choose to see the middle of a play or read the third part of a book. Or we might decide to follow with our eyes a drop of sweat as it runs down the face of a boring companion. This is what is meant by arbitrariness – focusing on the accidental, non-essential characteristics of any experience. To do so is to break with habitual modes of conscious apprehension and in doing so to reformulate one's entire experience of life.

Bull thinking, contrarianism, complexity, arbitrariness – these are all variations on a theme, different ways of putting into words the idea that we ought to strive to see and think *differently*. It's a world away from our usual concerns with IQ, EQ, SATs, GMATs, and suchlike. It's something we don't routinely measure, and if we did we would probably get it wrong. What the likes of Simonton and

Suedfeld show in their research – and what the likes of Paulson and Lahde show in their worldly success – is that it matters. And if seeing and thinking differently not only helps us to live more successfully but also with more gusto and *joie de vivre*, what objection could we have to that?

6

ENLARGING
EXPERTISE

The Nature of Genius

In 1988, Arthur Jensen, an academic from the University of California, Berkeley, arrived at Stanford University to observe a remarkable demonstration.[1]

Jensen had come to watch a woman named Shakuntala Devi. Born in Bangalore, India, in 1940 to a father who worked as a circus acrobat and magician, Devi had started out as a travelling stage performer. She had been invited to Berkeley, however, to show off her skills as a calculating prodigy.

Jensen already knew something of Devi's facility with numbers. An early article in the *New York Times* reported that Devi had added four numbers (25,842,278 111,201,721 370,247,830 55,511,315) and multiplied the result by another (9,878) to get the correct answer (5,559,369,456,432) in twenty seconds or less. A year after that, Devi had appeared at Southern Methodist University to show off some more. This time she extracted the 23rd root of a 201-digit number in just fifty seconds. (To give some idea of just how difficult that calculation is, Devi's answer had to be confirmed by calculations done on a U.S. Bureau of Standards computer that had been specially programmed to cope with it.) By the early eighties, Devi had sealed her place in history by making an entry in the *Guinness Book of World Records*. Her achievement this time? She had correctly multiplied two 13-digit numbers picked at random by the Computer Department of Imperial College, London. Those two numbers were 7,686,369,774,870 and 2,465,099,745,779. Multiply them and you get 18,947,668,177,995,426,462,773,730. The calculation took Devi just twenty-eight seconds.

It wasn't just idle curiosity that brought Jensen to Stanford that day to watch Devi at work. He wanted to see whether her astonishing skills could be substantiated in front of an audience of mathematicians, engineers, and computer experts. And – if so – he wanted to see whether he could persuade her to participate in some tests of his own.

Questions from those attending the demonstration – many of whom were armed with electronic calculators and printouts of problems they had submitted previously to the University's mainframe computer – were written on the blackboard by volunteers. Jensen copied the problems from the blackboard as they were written out; his trusty wife held a stopwatch to measure the solution times.

The psychology professor from Berkeley was not to be disappointed. For the entire performance, every single solution was presented in less than one minute (and most in a matter of seconds). For solutions involving really large numbers, Devi would write the answer on the blackboard; smaller numbers she would simply read out. Most of the problems were solved even before Jensen had a chance to write them down in his notebook.

When Jensen's turn came, he was ready. He had prepared two problems: 'What is the cube root of 61,629,875?' and 'What is the 7th root of 170,859,375?' The two problems were presented on separate cards because Jensen had (quite reasonably) anticipated that Devi would want to solve them one by one. But Devi was better than Jensen could ever have expected. She held up the two cards side by side and glanced at them briefly. 'The answer to the first is 395 and to the second is 15, right?' She had solved the two immensely difficult calculations not only immediately but also simultaneously.

Devi's real specialty, in fact, turned out to be roots. To 'warm up' she requested cube root problems, which she answered in an average time of six seconds. Ridiculously large numbers might slow her down: she did the 7th root of 455,762,531,836,562,695,930,666,032,734,375 in a painfully slow (for her) time of forty seconds. Irrational roots she just didn't like: the 9th root of 743,895,212 wasn't something that Devi wanted to be troubled with, it being the irrational number 9.676616492. (Devi dismissed it as a 'wrong number'.) With these exceptions, the correct number just 'falls out' for her.

———

When we come across people with truly exceptional abilities – people like Shakuntala Devi – we naturally conclude that we have discovered something like 'genius'.

That works for us in a couple of ways. It gives recognition where recognition is due: there's no doubt that people like Devi truly *are* in possession of something special, and it would be plain ungenerous to attempt to deny that. And it inspires us by showing what humans are – at their best – capable of achieving.

All the same, isn't there something else lurking behind the term 'genius'? When we take someone with some exceptional talent – be it a Mozart, a Shakespeare, or a Devi – and we label that someone a 'genius', don't we in some way also seek to relieve ourselves from any responsibility to reach similar heights? If another person is someone just like us but better, we struggle to emulate that person. But if that person is a *genius* – if that person is so far beyond us that they essentially fall into a category of their own – then we let it go. We forget about it: why fight an unwinnable war?

———

There could be no doubt that Shakuntala Devi was a truly remarkable woman. But – and this is the crux – wouldn't she be, perhaps, a bit *odd*? Wouldn't she be in some way fundamentally different from the rest of us?

Jensen thought not. Devi was, he said, alert, extroverted, affable, and articulate. She had excellent English and could speak several other languages. Among strangers she was at ease, outgoing, and self-assured, as well as being an engaging conversationalist. There was nothing out of the ordinary in her family circumstances, either, and none of her relatives had ever shown any unusual mathematical talent. A battery of elementary cognitive tests confirmed his assessment: Devi's general performance and reaction times were unexceptional. She was a completely normal woman with a completely exceptional talent – an enigma wrapped in a mystery.

The fact that Devi's abilities fell within the normal

range – added to the fact that she appeared to be an otherwise 'normal' person – raises the possibility that she *was* a normal person. Could it be that she was great at what she did not because she was intrinsically brilliant but instead because she just happened to be approaching it in the right way? And – if so – wouldn't it tell us something really valuable if we knew (even in broad terms) what that right way actually was?

LIFE SPAN PRODUCTIVITY AND DELIBERATE PRACTICE

In recent years the explanation for high performance has tended to focus on what can best be termed 'grind' – sheer number of hours spent. Malcolm Gladwell, famously, has popularized what, in its earliest form, has been called the 'ten-year rule'. The ten-year rule is a principle that governs the acquisition of expertise, and it tells us one very simple truth: you can't become an expert in less than ten years. (Gladwell's version is more refined than this and specifies 10,000 hours rather than ten years – but we'll come back to that later.)

Let's start with chess. It has been shown that the time taken between learning the rules of chess and attaining international chess master status is 11.7 years for those who learn chess late, and still longer for those who learn it early. Even the very best of the best

– prodigies such as Bobby Fischer and Salo Flohr – only managed beat the ten-year rule by less than a year.

Now consider music. Musicians who learn early have a definite head start, but even they cannot beat the ten-year rule: for those who begin at the age of six years or younger, it takes an average of 16.5 years before they create an eminent work, and for those who start later it takes just over twenty.

For scientists and poets the same basic rule seems to apply – no great achievements until at least ten years have been spent in the field. That's what E. A. Raskin found when he studied the 120 most important scientists and 123 most famous poets and authors of the nineteenth century. The average age at which poets and authors published their first work, he discovered, was 24.2 – but the average age at which they produced their greatest work was 34.3. For scientists, the average age at which they published their first work was 25.2, and the average age at which they produced their greatest work was 35.4. The numbers are uncanny: in each case it is just a month or two over the ten-year mark before true achievements are realized.

———

For the more precise version of the ten-year rule, however, we've got to look at the more recent research carried out by psychologist K. Anders Ericsson and his colleagues. Ericsson studied three groups of violinists from the Music Academy of West Berlin (Hochschule der Kuenste). The first group comprised the 'best violinists' – they had been nominated by their professors as those having the potential for careers as international soloists. The second group was composed of the 'good violinists', also nominated as such by their professors and matched for age and sex against the best violinists. The final group consisted of the 'music teachers' from the academy's department of musical education (which had lower admissions standards). While very accomplished by any standard, the music teachers would be unlikely to make careers as successful international soloists.[2]

In most respects the membership of these three groups was similar. Each group was composed of seven women and three men. The mean age of the young violinists was just over twenty-three years. They had, on average, started lessons when they were eight and decided to become musicians around about the age of fifteen. By the age of twenty-three, all the violinists had spent at least ten years practicing the violin.

So why were the 'best' violinists measurably better than the 'good' violinists, and why were the 'good' violinists measurably better than the music teachers? After all, they have all reached their ten-year mark. Doesn't this throw into question the ten-year rule?

Yes and no, it turns out – because although the ten-year rule may not always work when describing a precise 'ten years', it does work well as an approximation for 10,000 hours. The best violinists in Ericsson's study practised on average 3.5 hours per day and 24.3 hours per week. The weekly average of 24.3 hours multiplied by the 52 weeks of the year makes an average annual total of 1263.6 hours. The music teachers, on the other hand, practised an average of 1.3 hours per day – which would come to an average annual total of only about 475 hours. Remember that this would be cumulative year-on-year and you have at least one good explanation of the different levels of performance. At this rate, only the best students could break through the 10,000-hour barrier before they reached twenty.

So far so good. Why challenge 'grind' theory? If we need to grind away for 10,000 hours to achieve excellence, then so be it – 10,000 hours of hard grind it must be.

The first problem with the 10,000-hour rule, so presented, is that it suggests that there is some threshold point that is reached beyond which lie the fertile pastures of success: you put in your hours and – bang! – you reach a defining (10,000-hour) moment at which you have finally achieved excellence. That may be true for the relatively few areas of life that require expertise (narrowly defined) alone. But researchers who have looked at patterns of human achievement more broadly over the life span don't see it. What they see, typically, is a curve of productivity that does rise sharply in the first ten years, then peaks about twenty years in, but then drops off slowly for the remainder of the life span.[3] A curve like this:

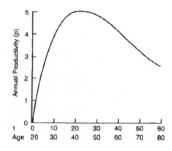

What's more, the curve differs according to the field in question.[4] Here are the productivity curves for the three broad fields of arts, sciences, and scholarship:

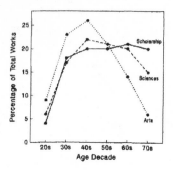

164

The curve for the sciences comes closest the Gladwellian vision: we see ten years of steady progress, followed by a leveling off after close to twenty (albeit with gradual decline later on). In the arts it's a more extreme picture: the career is more 'front-loaded' with rapid progress for the first ten to twenty years followed by an almost equally rapid dropping-off in productivity from middle-age. For scholarship, the story is different again. Our shabby academics, it turns out, are shabby for a good reason: they peak not after ten, nor twenty, nor even thirty years in, but a full forty years after they begin.

Problem two with the way that the 10,000-hour rule is sometimes presented is that it puts the emphasis on *grind* (i.e., on the number of hours spent) rather than *grit* (i.e., commitment to a single field of activity). The life span curves that we've seen above start with the assumption that our careers begin, uniformly, at the age of twenty: that's why we see the peak begin at between thirty and forty. What happens when we settle into a career at thirty, say? The curve shifts to the right by ten years. What happens if we start at thirty-five? The curve shifts to the right by fifteen years. It's not our biological age that matters; but neither is it simply how hard (how many hours) we have worked. What matters is how long we have been committed to a single vocation. What matters, to use the correct term, is our *career age*.

The final problem is that there has to be more to

it than the sheer number of hours spent. Some basic arithmetic reveals the issue: multiply *hours/day at your day job* by *number of days in the year minus weekends and holidays* and by *years spent working*. Do this calculation and you'll become aware of one feature that the 'expertise populists' rarely mention – even average human beings can clock up 10,000 hours after just a few years' work. Most of us probably work at least 2,000 hours per year. Work for five years at a single thing and we're all experts.

Of course, it's not that simple – because at the core of the 10,000-hour rule is not *experience* as much as *deliberate practice*. It has long been known that experience in itself is no reliable predictor of superior performance. Advice given by experts on stock-market investments is little superior to that given by complete novices. Psychotherapists with many years of experience are hardly more successful in their treatment of randomly assigned patients than psychotherapists just starting out. Expert wine tasters do little better than regular wine drinkers in discriminating and describing wines when the identity of the wine is unknown. In some fields additional experience is in fact *negatively correlated* with performance outcomes. Diagnosis of heart sounds and radiographs by general physicians, for example, actually decrease in accuracy and consistency with increased experience after formal training.[5]

Deliberate practice is a world away from 'mere

experience'. It's working at full concentration on improving specific aspects of performance. It's not execution or repetition of already attained skills but 'repeated attempts to reach beyond one's current level'. Typically it will involve the identification of weak points that are then systematically improved through focused efforts. It's not fun. It may be solitary. It will bring much in the way of failure and frustration and little in the way of immediate reward.

Here's how chess players do it. They get hold of published games of the top players. But they don't just study the games. They work through them, one move at a time, to see if their own moves coincide with those of the masters. If their selections match, then all is well. If they don't, then the player concludes that they must have made some error in planning or evaluation. It's at that point that the aspiring chess expert gets to work trying to understand the reason for the chess master's decision. *That's* deliberate practice – and some players carry it out for up to four hours per day.[6]

And here's how the most promising young musicians do it. Like their less promising peers, they spend up to 60 hours per week on music-related activities. What differentiates the really good ones, though, is the amount of time spent in solitary practice – twenty-five hours for the best as compared with ten hours for the less accomplished. And what do they do in their solitary practice? They work with full concentration on improving specific aspects of their performance as identified by their teachers during weekly lessons. That too is deliberate practice – and (as with the budding chess experts) some musicians do it for up to four hours each day.[7]

THE NATURE OF EXPERTISE

All of which sounds, of course, very mechanical – and that's the real danger.

Enter Oxford University don Meriam Bilalic and two of his cognitive science colleagues. As a doctoral scholar in the Department of Experimental Psychology, Bilalic had been interested in exploring what is known as the *Einstellung* effect. The *Einstellung* effect refers to the harmful influence of prior experience on solving problems, and occurs because we tend to repeat previously successful methods even when they are no longer appropriate. 'The first idea that comes to mind, triggered by previous experience with similar situations, prevents alternatives being considered,' says Bilalic. Scientists had previously thought that experts may be more prone to the *Einstellung* effect than the rest of us because they have already mastered and automatized the procedures that are routine in their fields. If that is so, experts will be less flexible and creative than the rest of us.

Is it really true, then, that experts become more rigid and less creative as a result of their expertise?

What Bilalic and his colleagues did was to

challenge chess players of a wide range of abilities to solve a problem.[8] Chess players are ranked like this (in descending order): Grand Master, International Master, Master, Candidate Master (or 'Expert'), Class A, Class B, and Class C. Bilalic calls the Grand Masters 'super experts': at more than five standard deviations above the mean, they are the world's truly outstanding chess players. One step down comes what Bilalic calls the 'ordinary experts' – the International Masters, Masters, and Candidate Masters – at three to five standard deviations above mean ability. Of course, you shouldn't underestimate their ability; normally an average player would have no chance at all of beating them. Finally come the 'ordinary players' – the Class A, B, and C players – at less than three standard deviations above the mean.

Bilalic now set a group of chess players – including no fewer than six Grand Masters – a chess problem. He presented them with the following board[9] and asked them to try to win the game in as few moves as possible:

169

In fact, there is a 'classic' solution to this game that is taught to all young chess players. It's called the 'smothered mate' because the Queen is sacrificed in order to draw one of the opponent's pieces onto a square that blocks the escape square for the King. In this case the 'smothered mate' solution would go like this (white to play). White Queen to e6, Black King to h8. White Knight to f7, Black King to g8. White Knight to h6, Black King to h8. White Queen to g8, Black Rook to g8 (taking White Queen). White Knight to f7. Checkmate in four moves. A good, solid, bluecollar solution.

There is, however, another – and more elegant – solution in fewer moves. It goes like this. White Queen to e6, Black King to h8. White Queen to h6, Black Rook to d7. White Queen to h7 (taking Black Pawn). Checkmate. Three moves instead of four. A better solution.

There's no need to get bogged down in the technicalities of the game. What matters is that the experiment demonstrated something very intriguing about the nature of expertise and excellence. Why? The 'ordinary experts' – all excellent players – were hit by the *Einstellung* effect. These players would have no problem finding the three-move solution when it was the only solution possible. (In fact, one of them on being told of the experiment commented: 'You will have to find a harder problem than this.') But when a more obvious solution presented itself – the familiar 'smothered mate' – they tended to fall back on it and miss the best solution. The most interesting outcome of Bilalic's experiment, though, is that the 'super experts' did *not* in fact succumb to the *Einstellung* effect. Every single Grand Master saw the optimal solution – and in an average of only seven seconds.

Here we have the crux of the matter – that 'super experts' see things differently. Specifically, they are highly conscious of solutions other than the obvious one.

Bilalic and his colleagues think that this is because super experts are able to 'chunk' information in the memory and use mental 'templates' that help them to be sensitive to even very small details in the context. But the theory shouldn't obscure the key difference between being good and being really good. The good players were able to identify a good solution and, once they had done so, settled with it. The *really* good players were able to identify a good solution – and then also identify an even better one.

––––––

You need some grind to be great at chess: you've got to put in the hours, and plenty of them. And you also need some grit: you've got to stick with it for years. But what Bilalic's work shows is something more intriguing than just that. It shows that the really top performers are able to absorb the routines and practices of their disciplines – and then go beyond them. You do your deliberate practice for years on end not so that you can master a narrow established technique – that's *Einstellung* – but so that you can *transcend* that technique.

THE MAGIC OF FAMILIARITY

Let's go back to Shakuntala Devi.

What's really special about Devi, it turns out, is much more interesting than anything that we could say about born genius or the sheer number of hours she has put in to cultivating her peculiar skill. What's really special about her is *the way she perceived her field*.

That's to say that numbers would appear differently to Devi. Consider, for example, the number 720. Contemplate it. Dwell on it. Toy with it. Do what you will – but for most of us the number 720 remains (stubbornly, obstinately) simply the number 720 and nothing more. Not for Shakuntala Devi. When Devi saw the number 720 (on a car license plate, as it happens) she 'read' it not as any old number but as 6 factorial (that's $6 \times 5 \times 4 \times 3 \times 2 \times 1 = 720$). She might see a four-digit room number as the sum of the cubes of two numbers or a stringing together of the integer roots of two numbers. If asked for the nth root of a certain number, she would, in addition to coming up with the correct answer, volunteer other interesting features of the number (e.g. it being the cube of one-half of the given number). Devi wasn't just calculating numbers; she was seeing the patterns by which numbers fold in upon themselves.

We can put that in a more comprehensible way. Take two simple sums, suggests Jensen. Let's start with $4 \times 23 = ?$ In general, we are reasonably quick with multiplications up to and including the number 12. That's because at school we tend to learn multiplication tables up to 12. However, get beyond the 12's and our response times are slowed. So even though $4 \times 23 = ?$ is a simple calculation, we can't do it as fast as we could do 4×9, say, or 4×11.

Now consider this calculation: $4 \times 25 = ?$ That one is *really* easy. There's no need for us to have ever memorized it as we may have done for other multiplications. We don't even need to actually calculate it as such. It's easy because we have acquired 'automatic facilitating associations' for this problem: we deal in hundreds and their fractions on a daily basis and we just *see* that 25 is one quarter of 100.

Could that be how calculating prodigies and top chess players see their respective fields? Devi's answer? It's a 'gift from God', she explained, 'an inborn gift'. And then: 'I think anyone could do it if they loved numbers the way I do.' So talent – almost certainly at least some. And love for the subject – that's evident too.

What really set Devi apart, though, was not necessarily – and certainly not exclusively – either of those. It was sheer *familiarity* with her chosen field. From the age of three when her fascination with numbers became apparent, her father began to teach her arithmetic. When she got good, he made her part of his stage show performing card tricks and calculations. And through all this she began to inhabit a world of numbers. 'Perhaps anyone could do it,' she has suggested, 'if they had played with numbers for hours every day since early childhood.'

DISPARATE FIELDS

It's an attractively simple analysis. And like most attractively simple analyses, it's still not quite right.

Look at the *fields* of achievement studied by the expertise people and you begin to see the problem. There's maths (or, more precisely, arithmetic). There's music (not musical composition but musical performance). There's chess. And there's sport. Each of these fields is a field in which what separates the high performers from mediocrities is the respective level of expertise. They are what researchers call 'standard talent domains'. In a standard talent domain, what you have to do to excel is to master an established skill-set and then employ it better than the rest.

What you don't have to do is to make a creative contribution to the field. A chess master, for example, works within the rules of the game to outperform his opponents; he doesn't have to rethink the nature of the game itself. A top violinist has to execute with precision and grace the music embodied in the score before her; she doesn't have to actually compose that music. Great sportsmen and women respond faster, harder, and with greater precision than lesser achievers within their respective sports. Nobody would expect them to pioneer entirely new sports. Can we safely assume that the development of a creator parallels the development of an expert?

When Dean Keith Simonton – whose age curves we have referred to above – came to review the literature on this, he was struck by the evidence suggesting that we simply cannot.[10] Creators have different character traits from experts: they are inclined towards 'nonconformity, unconventionality, independence, openness to experience, ego strength, aggressiveness, risk taking, introversion, and even psychopathology'.[11] But even more interesting is what Simonton found out about the development of creators over the life span. The most eminent classical composers, in one study, appeared to have spent *less* time in preparation than their weaker counterparts and had composed works for *fewer* years before making their first lasting contribution to the repertoire. The relationship between formal training and creativity, he observed, takes the form of an inverted U-shaped curve: more training increases creative productivity – but only up to a point, after which productivity declines. Even putting the extent of formal training to one side, creativity appears to obey its own laws: 'The ratio of hits to total attempts does not increase over the course of a career,' says Simonton, 'but rather tends to fluctuate randomly.'[12]

———

What, then, does it take to produce works of great beauty like these?

They are both works by Vincent Van Gogh painted circa 1882. The first is little more than a figure of a woman. Her head is bowed down into folded arms; she's clearly distraught about some personal loss the details of which we can guess but will never know. It's called *Sorrow*. The second is a lesser-known drawing of trees and tree roots battered and dragged by the winds that have blown into and across them for decades. It's called *The Roots*.

Van Gogh's life story does in fact tick all the boxes. He was born squat in the middle of the nineteenth century (1853) and died ten years short of the twentieth (1890). That's a calendar age at death of thirty-seven. But Van Gogh's calendar age was not the same as his career age because it was only when he was fired from his job as a minister in 1880 at the age of twenty-seven that his career began – so his artistic career lasted exactly ten years. And it was only after a full eight years into his career that he found his efforts were really bearing fruit and that he could finally execute an oil painting in one sitting: 'More than once,' he wrote, 'I have done a size 30 canvas in one day, but then I did not stir from the spot from morning till sunset except to eat a morsel.' The ten-year rule was something of which Van Gogh was painfully aware through his own hands-on experience. 'I am myself very, very dissatisfied with my work, and the only thing that comforts me is that people of experience say you must paint ten years for nothing,' he once wrote to his brother. 'It may have taken me ten minutes to draw something,' he would say at other times, 'but it takes ten years to learn how to do it in ten minutes.'

That ten years was well spent. Richard Brower, an expert on Van Gogh's life and work, describes how the artist mapped out his own plan.[13] Brower explains how he had noticed, as a researcher completing his doctoral dissertation, that Van Gogh had intentionally planned his activities over time so that his mastery would evolve in three stages. First, Van Gogh grounded himself in conventional art, before moving through a period of experimentation, until he had reached a stage of liberated mastery. He would begin by spending two years learning from his famous cousin Anton Mauve:

He started his career as an artist in 1880 at the age of

27. For the first 2 years of his development he devoted his energies to establishing drawing skills and learning basic techniques from Mauve.

Second, the next several years, from 1882 until 1888, he experimented with different approaches and emulated other artists, most notably the then renegade Impressionists and traditional Japanese artists. He spent 6 years of intense experimentation in an effort to develop a unique, personal vision.

Third, after serving an apprenticeship, and after experimenting with the knowledge he had acquired, Van Gogh liberated himself from previous styles of art, and learned to execute paintings quickly and effortlessly, so that a work that took him weeks to complete during the first 2 years of his 10-year tenure as an artist, took him 45 to 60 minutes to complete during the last year of his activities as an artist. He spent the last 2 or 3 years of his life executing work after work – sometimes up to three complete oil paintings a day, executed in an hour or less – in a style that was novel and that was a liberation from previous attempts by others.[14]

For Van Gogh as creator it was a decade not of semi-reluctant dilly-dallying but of thoughtful and self-directed training – and that's another aspect of the ten-year rule.

Artists share one other thing in common with experts: they repeat and revise and repeat until they can do it exactly as they wish. Leonardo Da Vinci sketched over a thousand hands before settling on the hands in the finished version of the *Mona Lisa*. Ernest Hemingway rewrote the ending of *A Farewell to Arms* a full thirty-nine times. Van Gogh was no exception: he drew over 150 heads before finally opting for the five heads we now see in his 'Potato Eaters'. In the words of one commentator, it was a kind of constructive repetition. That's not exactly the same as deliberate practice, but it's close.

So we have the years of dedication to a single activity and we have something akin to the deliberate practice identified by Ericsson. But there's one extra step that creators need to take that the experts don't: they need to be able to draw together and synthesize existing ideas to bring about something new.

———

Let's return to the career curves – but with a difference. This time, let's look squarely at one of the creative arts.

It's back to Simonton and (this time) the opera. Simonton was not interested in operatic performance – that would be a 'standard talent domain'. Instead, he turned his attention to operatic composition. That's a field in which technical expertise simply isn't enough. What's necessary to be a really great operatic composer is that elusive thing we call creativity.

Simonton looked at the careers of fifty-nine

classical composers and over nine hundred operas that they had composed. The operas were all rated for aesthetic success. (That's a composite measure based on the number of audio/video recordings, number of times the operas were performed in ten of the world's major opera houses, and number of times mentioned in histories, dictionaries, and reference works.) Simonton then applied statistical techniques to explore the relationship between the experience of composers and the success of their work. Would more years and more experience composing opera result in greater aesthetic success?

The results are complicated and intriguing. True it may be, shows the research, that the greater the number of years a composer has been composing operas, the greater their aesthetic success. However, look more closely and other trends appear to throw into question this effect.

One curious feature that emerges is that the relationship between number of operas composed and their aesthetic success is (broadly) negative. So, whereas composers tend to write better operas when they have spent many *years* working on opera, the actual *number* of operas they have composed tends to have a detrimental effect. On these principles, the composer who writes many operas is likely to be outperformed by the composer who writes one opera, produces no further operas for many years, and then finally returns to the field.

Another curious feature is that domain-specific

experience appears to have less impact on aesthetic success than broader generic experience. 'If a composer is working on an operetta, it is better to count the total number of *operas* he or she has so far created than to count the number of past *operettas*,' says Simonton. 'It might be better,' he adds, 'to count the total number of compositions of *all* types.' This isn't something we would expect if the simple expertise model applied. In the expertise model, if you wanted to become an expert at composing operetta you would deliberately practise operetta. Simonton's research suggests – counterintuitively – that you might do better composing violin concertos or cello symphonies.

So, for creators, does breadth of experience trump intensity of practice within a limited field? Almost right; but not quite. In fact, the greatest operas tended to be written *either* by those who specialized in writing operas (Rossini, Donizetti, Bizet, Wagner, Verdi, Puccini, etc.) *or* by those who showed exceptional musical versatility (Mozart, Tchaikovsky, Richard Strauss, etc.), with the latter group having an advantage. This mirrors the conclusions in a related study of over 200 scientists carried out by F. J. Sulloway which found that the most eminent were either extremely specialized or extremely versatile, also with the most eminent falling in the latter group.[15]

It's possible for us to excel in creative fields as in any other by working away in one narrow field until we are, effectively, experts. But in creative endeavour that's not the only way to get there, nor is it necessarily the best way to get there. That's because what characterizes the really top creatives is not their specialization at all; it's their breadth, and it's their versatility.

———

When Van Gogh had completed *Sorrow* and *The Roots*, he wrote to his brother Theo.

Van Gogh had been having a hard time of it. He had lost a lover: 'She for whom I felt what I wrote you about is not in my path,' complains the artist. 'She is out of my reach in spite of all my passionate longing.' And on top of that there were money problems. His works just couldn't be shifted: 'unsaleable' and 'without charm' were the words that were being bandied around. Van Gogh was forced to turn once again to his brother for help to the tune of 150 francs per month for another year.

It had been a rough time weather-wise too. Three nights of storm had ripped away the window of his studio where he had worked: 'You can imagine it was not pleasant. The wind came blowing across the open meadows and my window got it firsthand – the drawings torn from the wall, the easel upset, the railing downstairs also thrown down.' Van Gogh had been thrown upon his own and his neighbour's rather basic resources to fix the damage. 'With my neighbour's help I have been able to tie up the window, and I nailed a blanket in front of the hole.' No matter, concludes the artist: 'Before any success there must first come the hand-to-hand struggle with the things in nature.'

All he can offer is his work:

Now I have finished two larger drawings. First, "Sorrow" in a larger size – only the figure, without any surroundings. The pose has been changed a little: the hair is not hanging down the back, but falls over the shoulder partly in a plait, so more of the shoulder, neck and back is in view. And the figure has been drawn more carefully. The other, "The Roots", shows some tree roots on sandy ground. Now I tried to put the same sentiment into the landscape as I put into the figure: the convulsive, passionate clinging to the earth, and yet being half torn up by the storm. I wanted to express something of the struggle for life in that pale, slender woman's figure, as well as in the black, gnarled and knotty roots. Or rather, because I tried to be faithful to nature as I saw it, without philosophizing about it, involuntarily in both cases something of that great struggle is shown. At least, it seemed to me there was some sentiment in them, but I may be mistaken; well, you must judge for yourself.[16]

Look back at the two drawings and you can see it: something of that great struggle, as Van Gogh puts it. And that 'something' is something that has little to do with his ten years or his 10,000 hours and everything to do with cross-fertilization of ideas between different enterprises. Van Gogh could have spent his days perfecting how to draw a woman, or perfecting how to draw a tree. What he did instead was to work on both – and more. And isn't that the same thing that Simonton found with his composers and Sulloway with his scientists?

———

Why should any of this matter?

It matters because most of us really *don't* work in 'standard talent domains'. For most of us, the model of success is not the arithmetician, the violinist, or the chess player; the great majority of us do not have our lives determined by our expertise in a narrow field. Our work is far more likely to be characterized by fuzzy boundaries, opaque standards, and fluid, shifting goals. The problems we face may demand technical expertise, but our success rarely depends upon it.

Expertise theory has a lot to tell us about the need to knuckle down on a single path and the dangers of hopping from one enterprise to another. But that doesn't mean ten years to the exclusion of all else. If it means anything at all, it means ten years spent drawing together disparate skills and experience in pursuit of a single goal. And – in this respect at least – it's probably true to say that we're all a lot more like Van Gogh than we might ever have guessed.

7

THE
ACCUMULATION
OF ADVANTAGE

THE ACCIDENTAL CELEBRITY

It was early in 1990 when Mark Rowswell gave a performance that would, in due course, go on to make him one of the most famous Canadians the world has ever known.

It wasn't the first time that Rowswell had appeared on Chinese television. Just one year previously he had featured on a New Year's gala playing the role of a bumpkin in a comedy skit. It was a performance that was to give him his stage name, Dashan (coined because it's simple to write and 'a popular name for illiterate peasants'). But this time Rowswell was to do something a bit more than just turn up and play

187

the clueless foreigner: he was to perform a traditional Chinese form of comic dialogue known as *xiangsheng*.

Xiangsheng (or 'cross-talk') has been performed since the times of the Ming and Qing dynasties. Usually delivered in the Beijing dialect, it is a linguistically demanding art form, rich in puns and allusions. You can have one-man *xiangsheng*: that's a bit like stand-up comedy. You can have two-man *xiangsheng*: that's a double-act where one comic leads and the other chimes in. And if you want to make things really complicated, you can have three-man *xiangsheng*, where an additional comic is thrown into the mix to lead the others astray.

Rowswell's cross-talk debut on CCTV was a three-man *xiangsheng* called *mingshi gaotu* ('famous master – high student'). It was a curious event. In the late eighties China had little of the glitz and conspicuous consumption of today; there was still something very 'homespun' about the set and the studio audience. All the same, there was an air of mild expectancy to it all. The Chinese hosts were established comic personality Tang Jiezhong and Rowswell's very own *xiangsheng* master, Jiang Kun. Put these two together with a Mandarin-speaking Canadian and something amusing was bound to happen.

The fun begins. Rowswell turns up looking every bit the part: he's wearing spectacles, his sandy-blond hair is swept back to create a blow-dried *bouffant* effect, and (presumably as a concession to his audience) he's dressed-up in a black Mao suit. As he strides onto the stage, he's grinning awkwardly, conscious that this could all go horribly wrong.

The Chinese hosts introduce their guest. Then it's Rowswell's turn. It's the New Year and Rowswell wants to say a few words. His *xiangsheng* master, Jiang Kun, will translate:

> *Rowswell: Soon we will enter the New Year together.*
> *Jiang Kun: He says ... He is 24 years old today.*
> *Rowswell: I am very honoured to have this opportunity to say a few words to you all. [Rowswell bows deeply, touching his shoulder as he does so]*
> *Jiang Kun: He touches his shoulder ... It's a way of celebrating the workers.*
> *Rowswell: As we leave 1989 and enter the new decade...*
> *Jiang Kun: He says ... He's very tall ... and wears size 48 shoes.*
> *Rowswell: I would like to wish everyone the utmost success and happiness in the 1990s.*
> *Jiang Kun: He welcomes everybody to his house where he will prepare baozi [steamed dumplings] for them.*

The joke's on Jiang Kun, of course, who (like many of his generation) are too old to learn English but too proud to admit they don't understand. The audience are enjoying themselves; they all know people like this and there's the pleasure of recognition.

The sketch continues: the Chinese host has been

made a fool and now it's time for the foreigner to get his comeuppance. How? By making Rowswell perform a tongue twister in Mandarin. That sounds simple enough until you consider that Mandarin tongue twisters are based not just on words with similar sounds but on words with identical sounds and different tones. For example, the word for 'ten' (*shi*) and the word 'is' (*shi*) sound exactly the same apart from the tone of the former being a rising tone and the tone of the latter being a falling tone. The tones are one of the most demanding features of the language for a foreigner; it can take years to even properly identify the tones, let alone reproduce them.

Tang Jie Zhong runs through it first. The Chinese hosts then turn to their foreign guest. Rowswell must have rehearsed this but it's fairly evident that everyone's quite skeptical. Without a moment's hesitation he begins:

Si shi si [Four is four]
Shi shi shi [Ten is ten]
Shisi shi shisi [Fourteen is fourteen]
Sishi shi sishi [Forty is forty]
Shei yao ba shisi shuocheng sisi [Whoever says 14 in the wrong way]
Jiu da ta shisi [Then hit him fourteen times]
Shei yao ba sishi shuocheng shishi [Whoever says 40 in the wrong way]
Jiu da shei sishi [Then beat him forty times][1]

It's an immaculate performance, the likes of which the audience have never seen or heard before. The studio bursts into spontaneous applause and there are smiles all round. The foreigner can *really* speak Chinese.

The process that had been set in motion would make Rowswell a household name. Over the course of the following two decades, he would be transformed from stand-up comedian to TV presenter; from TV presenter to actor on stage and screen; and from actor on stage and screen to representative of his nation. Rowswell is now a celebrity and a household name.

It's an astonishing career for an ordinary chump from Ottawa.

———

What's striking about Rowswell's success is just how little of it appears to have been planned; he's truly what could be called an 'accidental celebrity'.

For a start, Rowswell is not obviously celebrity material. He is tall, blond, and not unhandsome – but that's where it stops. He wears spectacles. He has a goofy smile. When he stands straight, he stands a bit *too* straight. Rowswell gives the impression that he's not really comfortable with himself. If you met him on the street, you may suspect he was a computer programmer or an engineer; he has the look of somebody who would be happiest working with machines.

Then there's Rowswell's decision to dedicate himself to the Chinese language. This wasn't part of any grand plan; Rowswell simply found the other courses on offer 'kind of boring'. ('I didn't think it would hurt,' says Rowswell.)[2] His decision to go overseas was equally fortuitous: he applied for a federal government scholarship, got it, and went over in 1988 'with a sort of cavalier attitude just to see what would happen.'

And there's the show itself: nobody had a clue at the time how it would be received. 'Just close your eyes and shoot wildly and you just happen to hit the bulls eye,' says Rowswell of his first TV performance. 'That's really what that show was about and the producer thought this would be kind of fun. It was a New Year's Eve special; it's an international holiday, so let's get some international talent. Let's get a couple of foreigners in here to do a skit. That kind of thing is much more common now but in the eighties, there weren't a lot of foreigners appearing on Chinese TV and they were certainly not performing the kind of skit we were.'

Of all the stories in this book, Rowswell's is clearly the one most likely to support a 'randomness' theory of success. Rowswell just got lucky. China was already a decade into its 'open-up and reform' period; after years of self-imposed isolation the Chinese were finally opening-up to the outside world. If there had ever been a time and a place for a hapless Canadian to make an impact, this was it. Right place, right time.

Luck, though, can only be half the story. Rowswell didn't win the lottery. He didn't inherit unexpectedly. He didn't stumble across a pot of gold. His journey from unknown foreign student to national icon didn't happen instantaneously. There was a process at work: a process that transformed luck into opportunity and opportunity – inexorably – into success.

It's that process that this chapter is about.

HIGH ROADS AND LOW ROADS

When we talk about the success of the likes that Rowswell has enjoyed, what we're really talking about is the phenomenon of one (or some) individuals pulling away from the crowd. Unattractive as it may be, there can be no real success in this sense without some divergence: if we all succeed, then none of us succeed, because success is by definition relative. From a moral perspective, the crucial question will be whether or not the opportunity to diverge has been fairly spread. From a practical perspective, of course, our interest is a bit different: we want to know *why* and *how* such divergence occurs. And there's no better place to look for answers to that than in our schools.

American schooling attempts to be meritocratic.

It's not like Britain where a small number of private schools effectively train up an elite and feed them into the great universities. Nor does it have much in common with the European system, which channels a small percentage of students into academic secondary schools and then university while sending the rest to vocational colleges. What America attempts to do is to provide its young people with a general preparatory education, allowing students from all tracks to continue into higher education. The American school system has been designed to open doors rather than to close them.

But what actually happens to students as they go through the system? To find out the answer to that, you need data such as that provided by the National Center for Education Statistics (NCES), which has carried out a number of 'longitudinal studies', each following a defined cohort of students over a sustained period of time. One of them – the 'High School and Beyond' study – followed a national sample of 1980 sophomores, checking up on them every two years through 1986 and then one more time in 1992.[3]

The egalitarian bent of the U.S. system makes it harder to detect any initial 'head start'. You can't just look and see whether an individual has been to a private school, for example, or an academic as opposed to vocational college. All the same, there is one feature that stands out: the nature of the curriculum. That's because American students are still *tracked*: they are streamed on the basis of ability or curricular tracking, which continues, effectively, from high school into higher education. In twelfth grade, for example, some students get the benefit of courses in advanced algebra, geometry, trigonometry, chemistry, physics, and two or more years of foreign language taken from the ninth to twelfth grade. At the other extreme, some students get none of the maths courses, none of the science courses, *and* no foreign language courses. The rest of the students get the benefit of some of these courses but not all.

For convenience, let's call these three broad categories of students Group 1 (the more privileged), Group 2 (the moderately privileged), and Group 3 (the less privileged). Given that we know where our students have started out, it's now just a matter of checking in on them at intervals to see how they have progressed. In fact, we can do more than that: we can draw *career lines* that describe the students' passage through the educational system to college and beyond.

What we might expect would be a more or less random smattering of career lines. For example, we might expect some students to perform uniformly well and some students to perform uniformly badly. We would also expect some students to ace high school and flunk college, and some students to underperform at high school but then ace college. We would even expect some students to ace high school, flunk college, and then make a surprise recovery in later years. And we would of course expect to see some students – the 'B' students – performing at consistent if unexceptional levels throughout. In short, we would expect to see the full range of human variability.

That's not the way it turned out. Most of the cohort followed, in the words of one of the authors of the study, 'a few well-traveled career lines'. Out of 192 theoretically possible career lines (and 183 career lines that were actually possible), fully 52.5 percent of the students followed just *thirteen* of them. What's more, fully 29.2 percent followed just *four* career lines. Although nearly every career line was, in fact, followed by somebody or other, only a very small number of career lines were followed by a substantial proportion of students.

There is clearly a pattern here. So what is it? We need to look more closely at those four career lines that seem to draw such a disproportionate number of America's youth. They are these:

Student Trajectory	Tenth Grade	Twelfth Grade	Four Years Later	Ten Years Later
'Persistent High Road'	High curriculum	High curriculum	Four-year college	Further education in for-profit institution
'Short High Road'	High curriculum	High curriculum	Four-year college	[No further higher education]
'Consistent Low Road'	Low curriculum	Low curriculum	No postsecondary	No postsecondary
'Dropout'	Low curriculum	Dropout	No postsecondary	No postsecondary

What's striking about these four most commonly travelled career paths is that there's an obvious *bifurcation* into two 'roads': there's the 'high road' of early demanding curricula followed by further demanding curricula and then entry into a four-year degree programme – and there's the 'low road' of undemanding curricula followed by further undemanding curricula or a straightforward dropout from education altogether. If you expand these categories to include those whose paths were primarily 'high road' or primarily 'low road' (rather than exclusively so), then you find that 42 percent of the entire cohort have been channeled in one direction or another. There are far fewer middling performers than we might expect – and also far fewer erratic performers.

Alan Kerckhoff and Elizabeth Glennie, the authors of the study, see this as being a classic example of what they call 'cumulative advantage'.

197

Children in the twelfth grade who get the benefit of demanding curricula are not only likely to do better in the twelfth-grade tests of maths and English. They are also more likely to get into a better position (a four-year or private college, say) four years and even ten years out. Advantage heaps upon advantage: a good start gives the children a capacity to do well which carries them through to the next opportunity, which gives them a further capacity to do well – and so on. All this occurs even when factors like social background and prior academic achievements are taken out of the equation. It's not a result of family privilege or even innate ability – it's a purely *positional* effect.

What's more, the effect can be quantified. Imagine each child in the cohort is in a 'hierarchy of achievement', which can be represented by percentiles: the middling child is at the fiftieth percentile, for example, the truly exceptional child is at the ninety-ninth percentile, and the underperforming child is down at around the twentieth percentile. Once you've got these starting percentiles, you're able to calculate the 'deflection' caused to each child's percentile rank in the hierarchy by these positional effects. The scale of the deflections will reflect the scale of any cumulative advantage.

The amount of deflection between the tenth and the twelfth grade is noticeable but modest: 10 percent of the cohort were deflected downwards by at least six percentile points and 10 percent were deflected upwards by at least eight percentile points. Look at the deflection at ten years out and it's a different matter. More than 10 percent had been deflected downwards by twenty percentile points or so – and more than 10 percent had been deflected upwards by more than twenty-five percentile points. At this ten-year point, the child who had benefited the most was deflected upwards 27.9 percentile points, whereas the child who lost the most was deflected downwards by 24.2 percentile points – a difference of more than fifty percentile points. That means that the effects resulting simply from a difference in curriculum at tenth grade are enough to propel an average child into the top quartile or, likewise, send the same average child spinning down into the *bottom* quartile.

These figures are just what we would expect if cumulative advantage were at work. Relatively small initial advantages – studying algebra and geometry at twelfth grade, say – snowball into frankly astonishing differences ten years down the line. And the longer the period we look at, the greater the dispersal appears to be.

CUMULATIVE ADVANTAGE

The theory of cumulative advantage attempts to answer a big and important question: why is it that people who start out with more or less the same skills and qualifications end up with such disparate outcomes? Of two young science PhDs, why should one end up a Nobel laureate and the other a teacher in a third-tier school? Of two young lawyers, why should one end up on the Supreme Court bench and the other chasing ambulances? Or of two young actors, why should one end up on the big screen and the other waiting tables? In each case: was any initial difference in ability or potential really *so* great as to justify the inequality in outcome?

This is the question that was addressed by a man called Robert Merton of Columbia University. Merton's own career had been little short of stellar: born as Meyer R. Schkolnick, the child of East European Jewish immigrants in working-class Philadelphia, by the end of his life he had been granted honorary degrees by no fewer than twenty universities, including Harvard, Yale, Columbia, Chicago, and Oxford. Merton's immediate interest was the divergence of outcomes in the scientific world, and he looked to interviews with Nobel laureates – as well as diaries, letters, notebooks, scientific papers, and biographies – to find the answer.

What interested Merton in the first instance was something potentially very trivial: he noticed that when scientists collaborated – as they often do – it would be the better-known scientists who would get the credit: 'You usually notice the name that you're familiar with,' said one laureate. 'Even if it's last, it will be the one that sticks.' That doesn't seem surprising until you follow through on the consequences, as Merton did. Say Scientist A and Scientist B collaborate on a project. Scientist A is more famous than Scientist B. The project is a great success. Scientist A gets the credit – after all, Scientist A must have done the bulk of the work, we think, being the more eminent – and becomes even more famous. Merton's contribution was to show how this sets in motion a positive feedback effect: Scientist A just keeps getting more famous – and keeps getting more credit. And so on.

Cumulative advantage describes a similar positive feedback process but goes beyond distribution of credit to distribution of resources and opportunities. Run through the process again – only substitute 'resources' for 'credit' – and see where it gets to this time. Scientist A is identified as having star potential as a mere undergraduate; he is picked up by an Ivy League graduate school; with the support of eminent faculty, his graduate thesis garners attention from the research community; he gets a fellowship, fully funded, and a well-equipped lab; more good research; and onwards and upwards. Scientist B, on the other hand, may have had a touch of star potential but it was never well recognized. He gets to a middle-ranking graduate school where he can do solid if unexceptional work supported by solid if unexceptional colleagues. There's funding but not a great deal of it; he has to teach a lot of hours, which diminishes the amount of time he has for research. His work attracts little attention; he gets little in the way of new funds and little in the way of promotion; which gives him little opportunity to produce the kind of work that *would* attract attention. And so on.

Accumulation of advantage has been identified in a broad range of activities. Careers within corporations follow a path-dependent cumulative advantage process: early success in the competition for promotion greatly increases the prospects of further promotion; early failure more or less rules it out. Many criminals have, in their early years, received 'negative pushes', which have triggered cumulative *dis*advantage processes through labeling and harsh punishment. The same mechanisms have been shown to structure the careers of film stars, Protestant ministers, and even Communist Party members.[4]

The disheartening thing about all this is that it tends to extract the living, breathing human being from the picture. We're at the mercy of a cold and impersonal process that will propel us forward towards a future of continually accruing advantage – or it won't. Even more disheartening, on the face of it, is that what determines whether we get 'locked in' to such a mechanism will, at best, be some early demonstration of promise; at worst it will be nothing more than the luck of the draw.

Or is that an oversimplification?

Harriet Zuckerman, who has studied the phenomenon in Nobel Prize–winning scientists, thinks that it may be. While cumulative advantage might be able to give people a head start irrespective of merit or hard work, that's not the only way it works. It's true that inequalities might unfairly open up solely on the basis of a whole range of 'functionally irrelevant' criteria such as race, sex, religion, or social class, says Zuckerman – but they won't open up *fast*. In fact, it's precisely when resources are allocated on strictly fair criteria – notably, competence for the job or task in question – that cumulative advantage *really* takes off. 'Disparities in performance grow especially rapidly,' says Zuckerman, when 'the advantaged have been selected solely on criteria relevant to high-level role performance.'[5]

THE SUCCESS STORY OF THE JEWISH PEOPLE

How far does cumulative advantage take hold in the real world beyond the highly structured environments of schools and colleges? How, if at all, does it play out on the grand tapestry of human history? Can it explain the relative success not just of individuals over the course of decades but of peoples over the course of millennia?

Enter Zvi Eckstein. Eckstein has been the Deputy Governor of the Bank of Israel, has taught at Yale, Carnegie-Mellon, and Boston Universities among others, and has published in the fields of labour economics, monetary economics, macroeconomics, and development. What's really interesting about Eckstein, though, is that he is one of the few world experts on Jewish economic history. If anyone can explain the mystery of the disproportionate performance of the Jews, it's him.

A truly disproportionate performance it has indeed been. Take the number of Nobel Prizes awarded as a rough measure of achievement. In the first half of the twentieth century, Jews won 14 percent of the Nobel Prizes in literature, chemistry, physics, and medicine/physiology; in the next half-century the figure rose to 29 percent. The Jewish people, however, constitute just 0.2 percent of the world's population. Two-tenths of one percent of the world's population is responsible for about 30 percent of Nobel Prize–winning work. The maths is simple: the Jewish people are punching above their weight, so to speak, by a factor of more than one hundred.

Nobel Prize winners, however, are by nature unrepresentative. What about ordinary Jews? The statistics are every bit as curious. Even back in the early years of the twentieth century – when agriculture was still the mainstay of developed economies – as many as 99 percent of Jews from countries as diverse as those of Eastern Europe, Russia, the United States, and Canada had left tilling the land for more promising things. By the end of the century, approximately 53 percent of adult Jewish men were in the professions such as law, medicine, and academia, as opposed to only about 20 percent of white non-Jewish men. On the other hand, Jewish men are significantly *under*represented in the construction, transportation, and production industries: only 6 percent of Jewish men are out there working as builders, truckers, and factory workers, in contrast to 39 percent of adult males as a whole.

Follow the census and similar data and you find two other mysterious features of the Jewish story. The first mystery is the speed of Jewish 'catch-up'. When Jewish immigrants reached America, they moved fast. In the first two decades of the twentieth century, it took less than six years on average for a Jewish immigrant to reach the occupational status levels of immigrants from Canada or Northwest Europe – and it took only about fourteen years to catch up with native-born whites. After just over five-and-a-half years in the United States, wages of Jewish immigrants were on a par with those of native-born Americans. What's more, the Jews weren't just making money and getting ahead in their careers; they were also getting themselves and their children educated. By the 1910s, Jewish immigrants were achieving higher levels of schooling than their native-born counterparts. By 1990, 71 percent of adult Jewish men were college graduates. (That compares with just 25 percent for adult white men.)

The second mystery is that there has been, effectively, a premium for being Jewish. By the mid-century, Jews had a 19.2 percent earnings advantage over non-Jews. What happens, though, if you control for other variables that might be responsible for this effect – living in urban areas, for example, or living primarily in the north? Jews still had an advantage (albeit slightly smaller) of 8.8 percent. The same phenomenon occurs into the latter half of the century. Jewish men earned around 16 percent more than other men of similar age, schooling, and location.[6]

Outcomes so disproportionate cry out for an explanation.

Eckstein thought that the answer was to be found, if anywhere, in the unique history of the Jews.[7] So he dug deep into the archives. On the one hand, there were the Cairo Geniza, a 200,000-strong collection of Jewish manuscript fragments found in the storeroom of the Ben Ezra Synagogue in Old Egypt. On the other hand, there was the Responsa literature, the thousands of written replies composed by the heads of the Jewish academy in reply to letters they had received from all over the world.

What Eckstein found was intriguing. There was no sign that the Jewish people had always been exceptional: in fact, prior to the middle of the first millennium, the Jews – from Eretz Israel and Mesopotamia to Egypt and throughout the Roman Empire – had (like their neighbours and hosts) been a primarily agricultural people. Nor did it appear that Jewish society had progressed in a slow and steady, linear fashion. Instead, what Eckstein found in the archives was evidence of a massive turning point in Jewish history squat in the middle of the first millennium. At that moment – and in spite of the fact that previously 80 to 90 percent of the labour force had been engaged in agriculture – the Jewish people simply *stopped farming*. By the end of the first millenium, in Eretz Israel itself only 20 to 30 percent of the population still farmed the land. In the other parts of the world to which the Jews had migrated (i.e., the Muslim Empire and Western Europe), there were as few as 10 to 20 percent and 5 to 10 percent, respectively, of Jewish workers involved in agriculture.

What had happened? It wasn't, contrary to common belief, that anyone had forced the Jews to leave the land. Eckstein found that there was very little in the way of coercion; Jews had been allowed to engage in economic activity of all kinds, including landholding and agriculture.

The Jews had – quite simply – become literate.

It had been one of those unpredictable sallies of world history that would have unexpectedly profound consequences. The story that Eckstein tells is one of a massive shift in Jewish practice that in outline went like this. First, a high priest ruled that teachers be appointed in every district and boys be sent to them. Then, the Pharisees took the lead within Judaism, causing the religion to shift from one based upon rituals, sacrifices, and ceremonies to one based upon reading and teaching of the Torah. Accordingly, synagogues were built throughout the Jewish world, one of their central functions being the teaching of the Torah. Then the yeshivah (school for study of the Talmud) at Jabneh organized the vast body of Jewish oral law and began to carry out the role of academy, high court, and parliament to the Jewish people. So began what can perhaps be considered the most sustained literacy drive in history.

Why did literacy matter so much? The obvious answer is that at the heart of Judaism lies the study of the Torah and the Talmud. Judaism is a textual religion and to do it properly you have to be able to read. The importance of education in Jewish life was such that, in an era of general protectionism and restrictions on trade (the so-called *hasagat g'vul*), teaching was to be a radical free market. 'If there is a teacher of children and another comes who is better,' went one ruling, 'the better teacher must replace the incumbent.' The other side of the coin was that this was not going to be a culture hospitable to the uneducated. The Jews had a word for them: the *am ha-aretz*. You were *am ha-aretz* if you did not know the Torah and did not teach it to your sons. To be *am ha-aretz* was to be an outcast in the Jewish community.

The newly literate Jewish farmers now faced a problem, however: they had equipped themselves with a skill that brought no benefits and imposed considerable costs. Here's the issue. If you were a Jewish farmer in the first to third centuries AD, your monthly wage would have been 24 to 48 denarii.[8] Your monthly bread expenses for your family would have been 10 to 20 denarii. The monthly rent on your house may have been affordable at 4 denarii, but your clothing wasn't (it would have cost 30 denarii). If you saved up enough – 100 to 200 denarii – you could make a capital investment in an ox or a cow. The real killer? The price of a book – perhaps 200 denarii. Education was a luxury you couldn't afford – unless you went into the trades and professions where your investment in education would pay off.

While literacy is of little use to subsistence farmers, it's highly useful in skilled occupations. A merchant who could read sale and purchase contracts, partnership deeds, and loan documents would, for example, be at a clear advantage over another merchant who could not. The Jewish craftsmen and merchants found that they could enforce sanctions – through the academies – on other merchants who failed to play by the book. Even better, literacy enabled the Jewish merchants and traders to migrate with fewer costs than ever before because it was no longer difficult to maintain business and family connections. The world had just grown smaller.

That would be true for all peoples – but there was one reason why literacy was especially advantageous for the Jewish people. The Jews have not, for the most of their history, had centralized political power. They have lived in foreign countries where their rights over property and wealth have been dependent on the whims of local rulers and the laws of alien people. When you can't be sure of your rights over property the safest thing to do is to invest in human capital. Human capital is portable and it's inalienable. If circumstances change and you have to move on, you can take it with you. Literacy was a *safe investment*.[9]

From now on it's a story of cumulative advantage. As the Muslim Empire takes off economically, the Jews engage disproportionately in the trade and commerce that would service its needs. They move to the cities and find that the returns on their education exceed anything they could have hoped for as farmers. They have the resources now to invest in their children – and they do just that. And so the success story of the Jewish people begins.

The Jewish story replays what we have seen on an individual level in American schools. A smallish event, almost a quirk in history, is the beginning of a snowballing process that expands and entrenches a form of advantage. Can others catch up? There's no reason why not – but it becomes harder as the snowball gathers in size and speed. Once started, says Eckstein, 'this process will feed upon itself'.

SERENDIPITY IN PRACTICE

We humans have a natural bias towards linearity; chart progress on a y-axis against time on an x-axis and we expect to see a nice straight line. What cumulative advantage shows, though, is something quite different: career trajectories for the lucky ones look much more exponential than they do linear. The career track of the winner is not a straight line but a shallow curve that at some critical point sweeps decisively upwards.

———

Have a brief look at Rowswell's *curriculum vitae* and you get the picture:

1984
Rowswell commences studies at the University of Toronto and enrolls on a Chinese course because the other options were 'kind of boring'.

1988
Rowswell is awarded a full scholarship to study Chinese in Beijing; he makes his first appearance on television there.

1989
Rowswell becomes the first foreigner to be formally accepted into the *xiangsheng* hierarchy as a member of the ninth generation of performers.

1990s
Rowswell appears regularly across multiple television

channels as freelance host.
Time magazine selects Rowswell as one of the
'Leaders for the 21st Century'.

2005
Rowswell plays the lead role in a twenty-four-part
television series based on the life of the eighteenth-
century Italian Jesuit painter Giuseppe Castiglione.

2006
Rowswell plays the lead role in a stage play based on
the life of American reporter Edgar Snow, *Red Star
Over China*.

2007
Rowswell stars in a stage adaptation of the French
comedy *Le Diner de cons* (*The Dinner Game*).
Ford names Rowswell spokesperson for its Chinese
advertising campaign; Rowswell becomes the face of
the motor company's Chinese-language television,
radio, print, and online advertising.

2008
Rowswell is selected to serve as Canadian Team
Attaché and official torch bearer for the 2008
Olympic Games in Beijing.
Rowswell is awarded the White Magnolia Award for
Best Supporting Actor for his role in *The Dinner
Game* (the first time a foreign national has received
one of China's top three arts awards).
Rowswell is appointed to the Order of Canada.

2009

The Canadian government appoints Rowswell as Canada's Commissioner General for Expo 2010 in Shanghai.

Rowswell once again appears on the world's most watched television event to perform *xiangsheng*.

━━━━━━

This isn't exactly a linear career progression. It's jumpy. Rowswell starts out as a regular student in Canada, enrols on a few courses at Toronto University, then obtains a scholarship to study overseas. So far, so ordinary. Then comes the big break – Rowswell's first few television appearances. These launch him into the media and a career of regular TV appearances that will carry him for the next decade.

Then – more than ten years on from the initial break – comes the next leap when Rowswell gets to play the lead role in a substantial television drama. Suddenly you see a change of direction and a new burst of activity. From television drama Rowswell moves on to stage drama and advertisements; from stage drama and advertisements to Olympics preparation work; and from there to a role as Commissioner General for his nation.

That's precisely what cumulative advantage is all about. Cumulative advantage doesn't give rise to steady, incremental progress. It gives rise instead to

213

'turning point' moments at which a career just takes off.

For Rowswell, the first big break – the TV appearance – brought him a double advantage. On the one hand, it made him famous across a country of more than a billion citizens. From then on, Rowswell was a valuable commodity. He could be brought out for anything and benefit from the recognition factor – and each time he was brought out he would become still more recognizable and therefore still more valuable.

The second advantage may have been more subtle but more profound – something akin to what the children in the NCES study must also have benefited from. In Rowswell's first television appearance, he is stiff as cardboard. Apart from his language skills, there must have been little to tell between him and the next student. But then – each time he appeared on TV – he gained some confidence and some skills and lost some of the awkwardness. By the time he was appearing to critical acclaim in classic French stage plays and television dramas, Rowswell was already an accomplished performer. And by 2005, when he appeared as Giuseppe Castiglione, he had already cemented an advantage that would be virtually impossible for a 1988 classmate (without Rowswell's experience) to surpass.

WHEN OPPORTUNITY COMES CALLING

Cumulative advantage teaches us a few important things.

First, how far we get will depend upon whether we can trigger the phenomenon in the first place. Winners in the game of cumulative advantage are those who are able to lock themselves in to a positive upward cycle – those who find or land in positions from which achievement is rewarded not just by cold hard cash but by further opportunities for recognition and development. It's true that sometimes this may be an accident of birth; it's equally true that it may sometimes result from a lucky break. Often it means moving early and it means moving fast: cumulative advantage, as we have seen, isn't always a friend to the late bloomer.

Second, we've got to be ready to recognize and act upon cumulative advantage when it comes calling. What Rowswell's career shows us is one element of cumulative advantage: the power of publicity and reputation. It's not enough just to be good at something – all that means is that you will be good at that thing the next time too, and there's nothing 'cumulative' about that. What really triggers the process is to be *known* to be good at something – because that increases the chances you will be called upon to do the same thing (or something related or something better) in the future. Each time that happens you learn a little more and perform a little better – and become a little better known.

The really notable examples of cumulative advantage, though, tend to arise when the benefits that come from reputation converge with the acceleration that comes from *learning*. The children in the NCES study are testimony to that, as, on a more profound level, are the achievements of the Jewish people. When we say 'learning', we're not necessarily talking about 'education': once learning is standardized and widely available, it tends to lose its power to entrench advantage. What we're talking about is learning that's hard to get. Nowadays that probably means experiential learning: learning *how* more than learning *what*.

We know the outcome of cumulative advantage isn't exactly fair – what is? – but we also know that the benefits accrue primarily to those who are able to use the opportunities it brings most effectively. The final secret of cumulative advantage is that it's precisely when it's meritocratic that it takes real effect; the really sweeping advantages are reaped only when opportunity and advantage meet with ability and preparedness. The great irony, and the great challenge for us all, is to face up to the fact that the fairer the competition, the more unequal the outcomes may turn out to be.

CONCLUSION

The focus of this book has been on 'generativity' rather than the more obvious (but also more dubious) topic of 'success'. There is a reason for this: ultimate life outcomes are largely outside our own control. Opportunity, good health, economic security, and political stability are not available to all of us in equal measure, and even if they were, we would have no guarantee of their continuance. When we talk about generativity, on the other hand, we are talking not about outcomes but about principles, practices, and positioning – a person's ability to generate positive change.

———

What we can do here is to extrapolate from the conclusions we have been able to draw throughout this book. Assuming those conclusions are themselves correct, two questions arise. First, what kind of person is likely to be of the highly generative

type? And second, what kind of steps would one take
to become such a person?

———

Our highly generative person would, as a starting
point, manifest what could best be described as inner
freedom. While there is no doubt that highly
generative individuals have been able to change the
world, the first step for them would usually be to turn
inward and work on themselves. Inner state
determines experience of reality, which in turn feeds
back to affect inner state. Freedom comes from
recognizing that the key element in this cycle is, with
some practice and a little effort, within our own grasp.

The second characteristic that highly generative
individuals tend to display is the ability to marshal
their own energy. We have seen how we all have an
inner resource that can easily be depleted. This
resource is the one we call upon when we need to
exercise self-control, suppress thoughts or emotions,
and make choices. Generative people recognize that
this energy is limited and know how to deploy it to its
best effect.

There is a 'psychic environment' that lies behind
the making of a generative individual. Highly
generative people have commonly been trained under
other highly generative people. In addition to direct
human contact, they tend to look back in time,

sometimes across centuries, for guidance and inspiration from their predecessors. It has been said that you are the average of the five people you spend the most time with. Highly generative people would probably agree.

Equally distinctive is the mind that the highly generative person brings to the work in hand: focused, engaged, undistracted. The generative person is, above all, *present*. This is achieved first of all by engaging in work at just the right degree of difficulty. For immense tasks, that right degree can be found when the task is broken down into smaller, doable steps. It is facilitated when pride and pleasure are sought not in the achievement as much as in the performance of the task itself.

Typically, as we have seen, the highly generative person thinks independently and is tolerant of complexity. This person may well be an outsider or a dissident, a reactionary or a rebel. The English poet John Keats once referred to a concept he called 'negative capability' – the ability to hold in mind contradictory perspectives without pushing prematurely for an answer. 'At once it struck me, what quality went to form a Man of Achievement. . . . I mean Negative Capability, that is when man is capable of being in uncertainties, mysteries, doubts, without any irritable reaching after fact and reason.' We've seen how not only thinkers but also leaders and statesmen, as well as successful practical men and women, tend to have developed this ability to an unusual degree.

The highly generative person develops expertise. The starting point here is time – 10 years or 10,000 hours. But that's only the starting point. True high achievers don't just invest time; they engage in deliberate practice, and work with full concentration on improving specific aspects of their performance. And for creative producers, they don't just dig deep – they also forage widely, taking and synthesizing sources of inspiration from all around.

And yet the impression some of these people give is of deep calm and acceptance of their lot. Whether knowingly or not, they are likely to be beneficiaries of a hidden law – the law of cumulative advantage. This law favours those who start well, but it also favours those who stay the course, as it is only by staying the course that advantage accumulates. *Rien ne réussit comme le succès*, as the French say. Nothing succeeds like success.

Maintain state
Determine your reality by controlling your inner state.

Marshal energy
Your energy is limited. Don't squander it on trivial matters. Employ it wisely.

CONCLUSION

Control context
Pay attention to your psychic environment.
It makes you. So do your friends, acquaintances, and predecessors.

Cultivate presence
Engage. Be present. Enjoy the process.

Think differently
Cultivate independence of mind. Embrace complexity. Appreciate arbitrariness.

Enlarge expertise
Put in the hours. Engage in deliberate practice. Experiment in other fields.

Welcome serendipity
Sometimes good fortune comes. When it comes, it snowballs. Enjoy!

———

'When I was a young man, I wanted to change the world. But I found it was difficult to change the world, so I tried to change my country. When I found I couldn't change my country, I began to focus on my town. However, I discovered that I couldn't change the town, and so as I grew older, I tried to change my family. Now, as an old man, I realize the only thing I can change is myself, but I've come to recognize that if long ago I had started with myself, then I could have made an impact on my family. And, my family and I could have made an impact on our town. And that, in turn, could have changed the country and we could all indeed have changed the world."[1]

NOTES

CHAPTER I

1. Ramiyar P. Karanjia, "Beyond Humata, Hukhta, Hvarshta," *Parsi Times*, March 17, 2012.

2. Quoted in Elaine Pagels, *The Gnostic Gospels* (New York: Vintage, 1989), 126.

3. Jalal ad-Din Muhammad Rumi, *Selected Poems*, trans. Coleman Barks (London: Penguin, 2004), 73-74; William C. Chittick, *The Sufi Path of Love: The Spiritual Teachings of Rumi* (Albany: State University of New York Press, 1983), 257 (M II 1505-07); *The Secret Meaning: Rumi's Spiritual Lessons on Sufism*, 6th ed., http://www.thesecretmeaning.com, 69.

4. Alexandra David-Neel and Lama Yongden, *The Secret Oral Teachings in Tibetan Buddhist Sects* (San Francisco: City Light Books, 1967), 55.

5. Sean Müller, Bruce Abernethy, and Damian Farrow, "How Do World-Class Cricket Batsmen Anticipate a Bowler's Intention?" *The Quarterly Journal of Experimental Psychology* 59, no. 12 (2006): 2162-2186.

6. Photographic images from Müller, Abernethy, and

Farrow, "How Do World-Class Cricket Batsmen Anticipate a Bowler's Intention?", copyright © The Experimental Psychology Society, reprinted by permission of Taylor & Francis Ltd, http://www.tandfonline.com, on behalf of The Experimental Psychology Society.

7. Daniel J. Simons and Christopher F. Chabris, "Gorillas in our midst: sustained inattentional blindness for dynamic events," *Perception* 28 (1999): 1059-1074; Mukul Bhalla and Dennis R. Proffitt, "Visual-Motor Recalibration in Geographical Slant Perception," *Journal of Experimental Psychology: Human Perception and Performance* 25, no. 4 (1999): 1076-1096; Bethany A. Teachman et al., "A New Mode of Fear Expression: Perceptual Bias in Height Fear," *Emotion* 8, no. 2 (2008): 296-302.

8. Amanda Gefter, "The Evolutionary Argument Against Reality," *Quanta Magazine*, April 21, 2016, http://www.quantamagazine.org.

9. Aidan Moran, "Cognitive Psychology in Sport: Progress and Prospects," *Psychology of Sport and Exercise* 10 (2009): 420-426.

10. Jay Caspian Kang, "The End and Don King: The Crumbling of an American Icon," *Grantland*, April 4, 2013, http://www.grantland.com/features/don-king-faces-end-career/

11. Norman Mailer, *The Fight* (London: Penguin, 2000), 179.

12. George Lakoff, *Don't Think of an Elephant* (Vermont: Chelsea Green Publishing, 2014), xi-xii.

13. Ibid., 16-17.

14. Jeremy Wilson, "How Muhammad Ali won 'Rumble in the Jungle' with rope-a-dope, video analysis and no sex," *Daily Telegraph*, 5 June 2016, http://www.telegraph.co.uk/boxing/2016/06/05/how-muhammad-ali-won-rumble-in-the-jungle-with-rope-a-dope-video/

15. Mike Tyson, *Undisputed Truth: My Autobiography* (London: HarperCollins, 2013), 40-66.

16. Tyson, *Undisputed Truth*, 40-66.

17. John A. Bargh et al., "The Automated Will: Nonconscious Activation and Pursuit of Behavioral Goals," *Journal of Personality and Social Psychology* 81, no. 6 (2001), 1014-1027.

18. Ap Dijksterhuis and Ad van Knippenberg, "The Relation Between Perception and Behaviour, or How to Win a Game of Trivial Pursuit," *Journal of Personality and Social Psychology* 74, no. 4 (1998): 865-877.

19. Margaret Shih, Todd L. Pittinsky, and Nalini Ambaby, "Stereotype Susceptibility: Identity Salience and Shifts in Quantitative Performance," *Psychological Science* 10, no. 1 (1999): 80-83.

20. Fedor Dostoevsky, *The Idiot*, trans. Alan Myers (Oxford and New York: Oxford University Press, 1992), 552-586.

21. Daniel M Wegner et al., "Paradoxical Effects of Thought Suppression," *Journal of Personality and Social Psychology* 53, no. 1 (1987): 5-13; Daniel M Wegner, "Ironic Processes of Mental Control," *Psychological*

Review 101, no. 1 (1994): 34-52.

22. Emile Coué, *Self Mastery through Conscious Autosuggestion* (1922), chap. 4.

23. Primo Levi, *If This is a Man*, trans. Stuart Woolf (London: Everyman, 2000), 102-119.

CHAPTER 2

1. Dean Keith Simonton, "The Creative Process in Picasso's Guernica Sketches: Monotonic Improvements versus Nonmonotonic Variants," *Creativity Research Journal* 19, no. 4 (2007): 329-344.

2. "Guernica: Testimony of War", PBS, http://www.pbs.org/treasuresoftheworld/guernica/gmain.html.

3. Awarded by independent raters.

4. Simonton, "The Creative Process in Picasso's Guernica Sketches: Monotonic Improvements versus Nonmonotonic Variants": 337. Reprinted by permission of the publisher (Taylor & Francis Ltd, http://www.tandfonline.com).

5. Simonton, "The Creative Process in Picasso's Guernica Sketches: Monotonic Improvements versus Nonmonotonic Variants": 339. Reprinted by permission of the publisher (Taylor & Francis Ltd, http://www.tandfonline.com).

6. Jean-Paul Crespelle, *Picasso and His Women*, trans. Robert Baldick (New York: Coward-McCann, Inc., 1969), 176-177.

7. Roy F. Baumeister et al., "Ego Depletion: Is the Active Self a Limited Resource?" *Journal of Personality and Social Psychology* 74, no. 5 (1998): 1252–265.

8. Mark Muraven, Dianne M. Tice, and Roy F. Baumeister, "Self-control as Limited Resource: Regulatory Depletion Patterns," *Journal of Personality and Social Psychology* 74, no. 3 (1998): 774-789.

9. Kathleen D. Vohs et al., "Making Choices Impairs Subsequent Self-Control: A Limited-Resource Account of Decision Making, Self-Regulation, and Active Initiative," *Journal of Personality and Social Psychology* 94, no. 5 (2008): 883-898.

10. Shai Danziger, Jonathan Levav, and Liora Avnaim-Pesso, "Extraneous factors in judicial decisions," *Proceedings of the National Academy of Sciences* 108, no. 17 (2011): 6889-6892.

11. Reprinted with permission of PNAS.

12. Roy F. Baumeister and Nawal al-Ghamdi, "Relevance of Willpower Dynamics, Self-Control, and Ego Depletion to Flawed Student Decision Making," *International Journal of Education and Social Science* 1, no. 3 (2014): 147-155.

13. Brandon J. Schmeichel, Roy F. Baumeister, and Kathleen D. Vohs, "Intellectual Performance and Ego Depletion: Role of the Self in Logical Reasoning and Other Information Processing," *Journal of Personality and Social Psychology* 85, no. 1 (2003): 33-46.

14. Mark Muraven and Roy F. Baumeister, "Self-Regulation and Depletion of Limited Resources: Does Self-Control Resemble a Muscle?" *Psychological*

Bulletin 126, no. 2 (2000): 247-259.

15. Wilhelm Hofmann et al., "Cooling the heat of temptation: Mental self-control and the automatic evaluation of tempting stimuli," *European Journal of Social Psychology* 40 (2010): 17–25; Kentaro Fujita and H. Anna Han, "Moving Beyond Deliberative Control of Impulses: The Effect of Construal Levels on Evaluative Associations in Self-Control Conflict," *Psychological Science* 20, no. 7 (2009): 799-804.

16. Alexandra Enders, "The Importance of Place," *Poets & Writers* 36, no. 2 (2008): 27-30; H.B. Levey, "A theory concerning free creation in the inventive arts," *Psychiatry: Journal for the Study of Interpersonal Processes* 3 (1940): 229-293.

17. Ibid.

18. C.B. Ferster, "Schedules of Reinforcement with Skinner," in *Festschrift for B. F. Skinner*, ed. P. B. Dews (New York: Irvington Publishers, 1970), 37-46.

19. Jean-Paul Crespelle, *Picasso and His Women*, trans. Robert Baldick (New York: Coward-McCann, Inc., 1969), 64.

20. Ibid., 97.

21. Vladas Griskevicius, Robert B. Cialdini, and Douglas T. Kenrick, "Peacocks, Picasso, and Parental Investment: The Effects of Romantic Motives on Creativity," *Journal of Personality and Social Psychology* 91, no. 1 (2006): 63.

22. Crespelle, is*Picasso and His Women*, 153.

23. Jennifer A. Richeson and J. Nicole Shelton, "When Prejudice Does Not Pay: Effects of Interracial

Contact on Executive Function," *Psychological Science* 14, no. 3 (2003): 287-290.

24. *Sayings of the Buddha: A Selection of Suttas from the Pali Nikayas*, trans. Rupert Gethin (OUP: Oxford, 2008), 154.

CHAPTER 3

1. Reprinted with permission of the Art Institute of Chicago.

2. R. B. Zajonc et al., "Convergence in the Physical Appearance of Spouses," *Motivation and Emotion* 11, no. 4 (1987): 335-346.

3. Nicholas A. Christiakis and James Fowler, "The Spread of Obesity in a Large Social Network over 32 Years," *New England Journal of Medicine*357, no. 4 (2007): 370-379.

4. H.A. Krebs, "The Making of a Scientist," *Nature* 215 (1967): 1441-1445.

5. Ibid., 1442.

6. Ibid., 1442.

7. Ibid., 1443.

8. John A. Bargh, Mark Chen, and Lara Burrows, "Automaticity of Social Behavior: Direct Effects of Trait Construct and Stereotype Activation on Action," *Journal of Personality and Social Psychology* 71, no. 2 (1996): 230-244.

9. Patric Bach and Steven P. Tipper, "Bend It Like Beckham: Embodying the Motor Skills of Famous

Athletes," *Quarterly Journal of Experimental Psychology* 59, no. 12 (2006): 2033-2039.

10. Ap Dijksterhuis et al., "Seeing One Thing and Doing Another: Contrast Effects in Automatic Behavior," *Journal of Personality and Social Psychology* 75, no. 4 (1998): 862-871.

11. Henk Aarts, Peter M. Gollwitzer, and Ran R. Hassin, "Goal Contagion: Perceiving Is for Pursuing," *Journal of Personality and Social Psychology* 81, no. 7 (2004): 23-37.

12. Dean Keith Simonton, "Artistic Creativity and Interpersonal Relationships Across and Within Generations," *Journal of Personality and Social Psychology* 46, no. 6 (1984): 1273-1286.

CHAPTER 4

1. *Leonardo: The Artist and the Man* (London: Michael Joseph, 1988).

2. Quoted in Bramly, *Leonardo*, 281.

3. Quoted in Bramly, *Leonardo*, 295.

4. Mihaly Csíkszentmihályi, *Flow: The Psychology of Optimal Experience*(London: HarperCollins, 1990). See especially 43-70, 72-77, and 203-208.

5. Quoted in Jamie Chamberlin, "Reaching 'Flow' to Optimize Work and Play," *The APA Monitor* 29, no. 7 (1998).

6. Doug Robinson, "The Climber as Visionary," *Ascent* 9 (1969): 4-10. Reprinted with permission.

7. Mihaly Csíkszentmihályi, *Beyond Boredom and Anxiety: Experiencing Flow in Work and Play* (San Francisco: Jossey-Bass Inc., 2000), 74-101.

8. "Being Bachar" and "Bachar Can't Sleep", *Rock and Ice* 166. For more on Bachar, see the documentary film by Michael Reardon, *Bachar: Man, Myth, Legend.*

9. Adapted from Csíkszentmihályi, *Beyond Boredom and Anxiety*, 96-97.

10. Joan N. Vickers and A. Mark Williams "Performing Under Pressure: The Effects of Physiological Arousal, Cognitive Anxiety, and Gaze Control in Biathlon," *Journal of Motor Behavior* 39, no. 5 (2007): 381-394.

11. Jacqueline Louie, "John Bachar," Outdoor Spirit Group magazine. Reprinted with permission.

12. Dan Ariely et al., "Large Stakes and Big Mistakes," *The Review of Economic Studies* 76 (2009): 451-469.

13. J.A. Easterbrook, "The Effect of Emotion on Cue Utilization and the Organization of Behaviour," *Psychological Review* 66, no. 3 (1959): 183-201.

14. Chris Englert and Raôul R.D. Oudejans, "Is Choking under Pressure a Consequence of Skill-Focus or Increased Distractibility? Results from a Tennis Serve Task," *Psychology* 5 (2014): 1035-1043.

15. Denise M Hill et al., "A Qualitative Exploration of Choking in Elite Golf," *Journal of Clinical Sport Psychology* 4 (2010): 221-240.

16. James M. Hargett, *Stairway to Heaven: A Journey to the Summit of Mount Emei* (Albany, N.Y. : State University of New York Press, 2006), 1-19.

17. Adapted from Zhang Chengye, *Mount Emei: Folktales*, trans. Hu Xiong (Chengdu: Sichuan People's Publishing House, 1986), 46-50.

18. Reprinted with permission of the National Palace Museum (Taipei) from the Collection of the National Palace Museum.

CHAPTER 5

1. William G. Perry, "Examsmanship and the Liberal Arts: A Study in Educational Epistemology," in *Examining in Harvard College: A Collection of Essays by Members of the Harvard Faculty*, ed. L. Bramsom (Cambridge, MA: Harvard University, 1963), 125-135. A copy can be found at http://www.people.fas.harvard.edu/-lipoff/miscellaneous/exams.html.

2. Gregory Zuckerman, *The Greatest Trade Ever: The Behind-the-Scenes Story of How Paulson Defied Wall Street and Made Financial History*(New York: Broadway Books, 2009). See also "Face Value: Long and Short," *Economist*, March 14, 2009, 62.

3. Dean Keith Simonton, "Philosophical Eminence, Beliefs, and Zeitgeist: An Individual-Generational Analysis," *Journal of Personality and Social Psychology* 34, no. 4 (1976): 630-640.

4. Your polar contrast index (or PCI) can be calculated as follows: PCI = PC/PC QC IC. A high PCI will suggest high levels of polarized thinking (relative to

more flexible forms of thinking) and therefore lower levels of cognitive complexity.

5. Peter Suedfeld and A. Dennis Rank, "Revolutionary Leaders: Long-Term Success as a Function of Changes in Conceptual Complexity," *Journal of Personality and Social Psychology* 34, no. 2 (1976): 169-178.

6. Peter Suedfeld and Philip Tetlock, "Integrative Complexity of Communications in International Crises," *The Journal of Conflict Resolution* 21, no. 1 (1977): 169-184.

7. Peter Suedfeld, Philip E Tetlock, and Carmenza Ramirez, "War, Peace, and Integrative Complexity: UN Speeches on the Middle East Problem, 1947-1976," *Journal of Conflict Resolution* 21, no. 3 (1977), 427-442.

8. "Face Value: The Long and the Short", 62.

9. Zuckerman, *The Greatest Trade Ever.*

10. Søren Kierkegaard, *Either/Or: A Fragment of Life*, trans. Alastair Hannay and ed. Victor Eremita (London: Penguin, 2004), 227-241.

CHAPTER 6

1. Arthur R. Jensen, "Speed of Information Processing in a Calculating Prodigy," *Intelligence* 14 (1990): 259-274.

2. K. Anders Ericsson, Ralf Th. Krampe, and Clemens Tesch-Romer, "The Role of Deliberate Practice in the Acquisition of Expert Performance," *Psychological*

Review 100, no. 3 (1993): 363-406.

3. Dean Keith Simonton, "Creative Productivity: A Predictive and Explanatory Model of Career Trajectories and Landmarks," *Psychological Review* 104, no. 1 (1997): 66-89.

4. Simonton, "Creative Productivity," 71.

5. K. Anders Ericsson, Roy W Roring, and Kiruthiga Nandagopal, "Giftedness and Evidence for Reproducibly Superior Performance: An Account Based on the Expert Performance Framework," *High Ability Studies* 18, no. 1 (2007): 3-56.

6. K. Anders Ericsson, "Expertise in Interpreting: An Expert-Performance Perspective," *Interpreting* 5, no. 2 (2000): 187-220.

7. Ericsson, Roring, and Nandagopal, "Giftedness and Evidence for Reproducibly Superior Performance," 17.

8. Merim Bilalić, Peter McLeod, and Fernand Gobet, "Inflexibility of Experts – Reality or Myth? Quantifying the Einstellung Effect in Chess Masters," *Cognitive Psychology* 56 (2008): 73-102.

9. Reprinted from Bilalić, "Inflexibility of Experts – Reality or Myth? Quantifying the Einstellung Effect in Chess Masters," with permission from Elsevier.

10. Dean Keith Simonton, "Creative Development as Acquired Expertise: Theoretical Issues and an Empirical Test," *Developmental Review* 20 (2000): 283-318.

11. Ibid., 285.

12. Ibid., 286.

13. Richard Brower, "To Reach a Star: The Creativity of Vincent van Gogh," *High Ability Studies* 11, no. 2 (2000): 179-205.

14. Ibid., 193. Copyright © European Council for High Ability reprinted by permission of Taylor & Francis Ltd (http://www.tandfonline.com) on behalf of European Council for High Ability.

15. Simonton, "Creative Development as Acquired Expertise," 311.

16. "Letter from Vincent van Gogh to Theo van Gogh" dated 1 May 1882. Leo Jansen, Hans Luijten, Nienke Bakker (eds.) (2009), *Vincent van Gogh – The Letters*. Version: December 2010. Amsterdam & The Hague: Van Gogh Museum & Huygens ING. http://vangoghletters.org. Consult the homepage for the current version.

CHAPTER 7

1. The original Chinese *pinyin* (with tone markers) is like this: si4 shi4 si4 [four is four], shi2 shi4 shi2 [ten is ten], shi2si4 shi4 shi2si4 [fourteen is fourteen], si2shi4 shi4 si2shi4 [forty is forty], shei2 yao4 ba3 shi2si4 shuo1cheng2 si2si4 [whoever says 14 in the wrong way], jiu3 da3 ta1 shi2si4 [then hit him fourteen times], shei2 yao4 ba3 si4shi2 shuo1cheng2 shi4shi2 [whoever says 40 in the wrong way], jiu3 da2 shei2 si4shi2 [then beat him forty times].

2. "Who Says You Can't Move Mountains,"

Intercultures Magazine, 2, no. 2 (2009), https://web.archive.org/web/20150422002459/ http:/www.international.gc.ca/cil-cai/magazine/ v02n02/1-2.aspx?lang=eng

3. Alan C. Kerckhoff and Elizabeth Glennie, "The Matthew Effect in American Education," *Research in Sociology of Education and Socialization* 12 (1999): 35-66.

4. Harriet Zuckerman, "Accumulation of Advantage and Disadvantage: The Theory and its Intellectual Biography," in *Robert K. Merton & Contemporary Sociology*, ed. Carlo Mongardini and Simonetta Tabboni (New Brunswick and London: Transaction Publishers, 1998), 139-161.

5. Ibid., 143.

6. Barry R. Chiswick, "The Occupational Attainment and Earnings of American Jewry, 1890 to 1990," *Contemporary Jewry* 20 (1999): 68-98.

7. Maristella Botticini and Zvi Eckstein, "Jewish Occupational Selection: Education, Restrictions, or Minorities?" *The Journal of Economic History* 65, no. 4 (2005): 922-948. See also M. Botticini and Z. Eckstein "Path Dependence in Occupations," in *The New Palgrave Dictionary of Economics* (2006).

8. In the Roman currency system, the denarius (plural: denarii) was a small silver coin, originally worth ten asses.

9. Dennis W. Carlton and Avi Weiss, "The Economics of Religion, Jewish Survival, and Jewish Attitudes Toward Competition in Torah Education," *Journal of Legal Studies* 30 (2001): 253-275.

CONCLUSION

1. Attributed to Rabbi Israel Salanter, nineteenth-century Talmudist.

INDEX

Also Available

Classic Philosophy for the Modern Man

Andrew Lynn

'*What you hold in your hands is a handbook for living: it is an account of how the greatest minds have spoken to us on how to grow and prosper as flesh-and-blood human beings.*'

Classic Philosophy for the Modern Man is inspired by a single concept: that, to thrive in the world, we need ready access to the practical wisdom of our forebears. It answers that need by introducing for the general reader the most powerful and enduringly relevant works of great thinkers from around the world. Together these works teach us how to achieve excellence; how to obtain and exercise power, advance in the world, and live gracefully; how to cultivate nobility of soul; and – above all – how to be one's own man. There is no better primer in the art of living well.

Made in the USA
San Bernardino, CA
12 December 2018